HISTORY OF THE
EAST INDIAN RAILWAY.

BY

G. HUDDLESTON, C.I.E.
Chief Superintendent, E. I. Ry.

CALCUTTA:
THACKER, SPINK AND CO.

1906.

This scarce antiquarian book is included in our special *Legacy Reprint Series*. In the interest of creating a more extensive selection of rare historical book reprints, we have chosen to reproduce this title even though it may possibly have occasional imperfections such as missing and blurred pages, missing text, poor pictures, markings, dark backgrounds and other reproduction issues beyond our control. Because this work is culturally important, we have made it available as a part of our commitment to protecting, preserving and promoting the world's literature. Thank you for your understanding.

Lambert Weston & Sons.

SIR MACDONALD STEPHENSON.
FOUNDER OF THE EAST INDIAN RAILWAY.

Frontispiece.

TO
MY BROTHER OFFICERS AND FELLOW WORKMEN ON THE
EAST INDIAN RAILWAY, PAST AND PRESENT.
THIS WORK IS DEDICATED.
G. H.

PREFACE.

It is not everyone who realizes what a great undertaking the East Indian Railway is, or what it has done and is doing for the people and the trade of India and particularly of Calcutta. Yet the author hardly ventures to expect that this endeavour, to outline the more important events in its history, will prove attractive to the general reader, or help him to an appreciation of the facts.

It is chiefly for those who are or have been associated with or employed on the East Indian Railway that this book has been written, and if these, as well as those who enter its service in the future, find something in its pages to interest them, the writer will be rewarded.

The author would only add that in attempting the work he has been prompted by a feeling that unless something was done now, to place on record facts which are so easily forgotten and so soon buried in oblivion, the opportunity would be lost. No one can be more conscious than he is of the many defects and imperfections of his effort, and had anyone else evinced a desire to undertake the task, he would not have set it himself.

PREFACE.

It is not everyone who realizes what a great undertaking the East Indian Railway is, or what it has done and is doing for the people and the trade of India and particularly of Calcutta. Yet the author hardly ventures to expect that this endeavour, to outline the more important events in its history, will prove attractive to the general reader, or help him to an appreciation of the facts.

It is chiefly for those who are or have been associated with or employed on the East Indian Railway that this book has been written, and if these, as well as those who enter its service in the future, find something in its pages to interest them, the writer will be rewarded.

The author would only add that in attempting the work he has been prompted by a feeling that unless something was done now, to place on record facts which are so easily forgotten and so soon buried in oblivion, the opportunity would be lost. No one can be more conscious than he is of the many defects and imperfections of his effort, and had anyone else evinced a desire to undertake the task, he would not have set it himself.

In saying this he hopes it will be distinctly understood that the production is on no sense official and no one but the author is in any way responsible for it.

His thanks are due to Mr. H. Wood, Secretary to the Agent in Calcutta, to whom he is indebted for the two chapters on the Provident Fund and the Hill School; to Mr. P. A. M. Nash, District Locomotive Superintendent, who kindly furnished the account of the Jamalpur workshops; to Mr. John Strachan, late Locomotive Superintendent, and to other friends whose assistance is acknowledged in the pages of the book.

CALCUTTA, *May* 1906.   G. HUDDLESTON.

CONTENTS.

CHAPTER I—   PAGE.

    Formation of the East Indian Railway—Original Idea to connect Calcutta with Delhi—The First Contract—Commencement of Construction—Opening of Line as far as Raneegunge ... 1

CHAPTER II—

    Progress of Construction—Effect of the Mutiny—Visit of Mr. A. M. Rendel to India ... 17

CHAPTER III—

    Opening of the Railway to Rajmahal and subsequently to Delhi—Retirement of Mr. George Turnbull, the First Railway Engineer in India—The Construction of the Chord Line decided upon—Unexpected Growth of Traffic, followed by Complaints of Want of Adequate Facilities... 28

CHAPTER IV—

    The Alignment of the East Indian Railway, and other matters ... 48

CHAPTER V—

    Trade Depression—Mr. A. M. Rendel visits India again and criticises the Working of the East Indian Railway—Establishment of a Provident Fund ... 57

CHAPTER VI—

    Opening of the Chord Line followed by a Temporary Slump in Traffic—The Bengal Famine of 1873-4—Reductions in Rates—Coal exported from Calcutta—Analysis of Statistics introduced ... 63

CONTENTS.

CHAPTER VII—   PAGE.

Visit of the Prince of Wales to India—Reductions in Rates—Economies in Working—The Madras Famine and Shortage of Stock—General Strachey visits India—The Giridih Collieries—Prosperity of the Undertaking 72

CHAPTER VIII—

Opening of the Rajputana Railway leads to Competition between Calcutta and Bombay—The Views of Government on the Question—The Position defined by Mr. Crawford, Chairman of the East Indian Railway 89

CHAPTER IX—

Negotiations preceding the Purchase of the East Indian Railway by Government 101

CHAPTER X—

Questions before the Board after the Purchase of the Railway by Government—Retrospect of the Position of the Company at the time—Reduction of Third Class Fares, and other matters ... 106

CHAPTER XI—

Growth of the Coal Trade in 1883—The Question of Working the East India Railway by State or Company Management—Agitation in Calcutta regarding Construction of the Grand Chord—Retirement of Sir Bradford Leslie—Death of Mr. Crawford 123

CHAPTER XII—

Appointment of General Sir Richard Strachey as Chairman—His visit to India 136

CHAPTER XIII—

The Grand Chord Line 141

CHAPTER XIV—

The Jherriah Coal-field 145

CHAPTER XV—

Coal Rates 151

CHAPTER XVI—
 Growth of the Coal Traffic 160

CHAPTER XVII—
 The Kidderpore Docks 169

CHAPTER XVIII—
 Train Service and Working Facilities—The Question of Wagon Supply 176

CHAPTER XIX—
 Some Further Remarks on Competition and Rates 184

CHAPTER XX—
 Third Class Passengers 190

CHAPTER XXI—
 Proposed Central Station in Calcutta 196

CHAPTER XXII—
 Provident Institution 202

CHAPTER XXIII—
 Hill School 208

CHAPTER XXIV—
 General Growth of Traffic 214

CHAPTER XXV—
 Various Projects for dealing with the Export Coal Trade, and other matters 220

CHAPTER XXVI—
 Statistics 229

CHAPTER XXVII—
 The Jamalpur Workshops 240

CHAPTER XXVIII—
 Outbreak of Plague—Immunity of E. I. R. from Serious Accidents—The Delhi Durbar—Mr. T. Robertson's Enquiry into Indian Railway Working—Removal of Carriage Shops to Lillooah 252

CHAPTER XXIX—
 The East Indian Railway under Two Chairmen. 263

HISTORY

OF

THE EAST INDIAN RAILWAY.

CHAPTER I.

FORMATION OF THE EAST INDIAN RAILWAY—ORIGINAL IDEA TO CONNECT CALCUTTA WITH DELHI—THE FIRST CONTRACT—COMMENCEMENT OF CONSTRUCTION—OPENING OF LINE AS FAR AS RANEEGUNGE.

IN May, 1845, or about twenty years after the construction of the first railroad in England, the East Indian Railway Company, was organised. The earliest report of the Directors to the Shareholders was not made, however, until nearly two years later; the interval having been passed in negotiations with the Honourable East India Company, and in the preparation of estimates of cost and of traffic, as well as in a survey of the country through which the proposed line would pass.

At this time, the Chairman was Sir George Larpent, the Deputy Chairman, Mr. Bazett D. Colvin, and the Managing Director,

Mr. R. Macdonald Stephenson. Of these, Mr., afterwards, Sir R. Macdonald Stephenson, may be said to have been the founder of the Company, for he it was who first introduced the idea of railroads in India, and advocated the construction of the East Indian line almost along the same route that it now traverses.

It was in July, 1845, that Mr. Macdonald Stephenson, accompanied by three well qualified assistants, proceeded to Bengal and on arrival in Calcutta commenced, in the Board's words, " with diligence and discretion which cannot be too highly commended, to survey the line from Calcutta to Delhi, through Mirzapore, and so great and persevering were the exertions of himself and Staff, that, in April, 1846, the surveys of the whole line were completed ; important statistical information obtained and an elaborate report transmitted to your Directors in London." All trace of this report, excepting only the statistics of cost and estimates of traffic has been lost, but it strongly impressed the Board with the conviction that a line from Calcutta to Delhi not only possessed political advantages of the highest order, but that it would also prove a success as a commercial speculation. The statistical information obtained by Mr. Stephenson, showed that although the cost of introducing an entirely new system of locomotion in a country such as India, was necessarily subject to some uncertainty, yet, there were good grounds for anticipating that the maximum expenditure on a double line of railway from Calcutta to Delhi, through Mirzapore, assuming that the Government would grant the necessary land without charge, would not exceed £15,000 per mile. It was also calculated that without any increase of the existing traffic, that is to say, of the traffic then forwarded by river and road, a large dividend might be looked for.

From the outset, the Court of Directors of the Honourable East India Company, shared with the Directors of the East Indian Railway Company, the view that the benefit to be derived by India from the introduction of a railroad system was beyond question, but circumstances in the political and monetary state of India were constantly changing, while there was no certainty of the London share market. Very great caution was therefore needed in conducting the preliminary negotiations for the construction of so great a national work, involving so large a capital outlay, in a country so distant and at the time so little known.

Terms were proposed in the first instance, which would now seem to have been sufficiently liberal, though the then Board did not think so, and ultimately obtained substantial modifications. The first conclusions of the East India Company, and what they were prepared to do towards the introduction of a railway system in India, may however be summarised as follows:—

1st. That it was deemed of great importance to connect the seat of the Supreme Government of India with the North-West Provinces.

2nd. That provided no serious difficulty, arising out of the physical character of the country, was found to exist, the line of the first Railway in India should be from Calcutta to Delhi through Mirzapore.

3rd. That the Honourable East India Company were prepared to sanction the construction of two sections of that line, one in the Lower and the other in the Upper Provinces; to grant the land for the Railway *free of all cost* for ninety-nine years; to advance interest at four per cent. per annum for fifteen years, on the capital to be employed on these sections not exceeding £3,000,000 sterling; to commence paying such interest so soon as the contract should be arranged, and to receive repayment thereof when the *profits* of the line should exceed four per cent.

After much correspondence these terms were modified, the chief points conceded by the East India Company being that the rate of interest should be raised from 4 to 5 per cent., and that the term during which this interest would be paid should be raised from 15 to 25 years. The revised terms were accepted by the Directors " with a grateful sense of the liberal manner in which they had been treated by the East India Company," and the belief was expressed that the undertaking "whilst it will prove a great blessing to the Empire, will afford the means of a safe and profitable investment to individuals."

It should here be mentioned, that other interests conflicting with the East Indian Railway Company had at this time to be considered; another Company had been formed, shortly after the East Indian, known as the "Great Western of Bengal Railway," for the purpose of constructing a line from Calcutta to Rajmahal, to be carried over a portion of the projected main line of the East Indian Railway, and entering into competition with the branch to Rajmahal, contemplated by that railway. It was considered expedient to amalgamate the interests of the two companies, and this was done on terms unnecessary to detail.

Towards the end of 1847, the Board having taken into consideration the arrangements best calculated to give effect to the Company's operations in India, came to the conclusion, that "the interests of the undertaking would be best consulted by the appointment in India of a Committee of gentlemen, independent of local interest or connection, and who should be entirely and wholly subject to the control of the Board in London," and in pursuance of this policy two gentlemen "of talent and experience" (Messrs. Adams and Beeston) were appointed to act, conjointly with Mr. Stephenson, as their representatives in India, and these three sailed to India on the 20th September, 1847, accompanied by a staff of Engineers carefully selected by the Company's Consulting Engineer, Mr. James Rendel, the father of the present Consulting Engineer, Sir A. M. Rendel.

So far, once preliminary negotiations had been settled, it had been plain sailing, but unfortunately difficulties now arose which took some time to overcome. Various documents both anonymous and otherwise were circulated, and advertised in the public newspapers and elsewhere, in which endeavours were made to prove that the proposed line could not pay, certain of the Directors resigned, and some of the proprietors delayed settlement of calls on their shares, with the result that financial difficulties followed, and the staff sent out to India had to be recalled.

In the meantime, there were renewed negotiations with the Honourable East India Company, which took up a couple of years, but ultimately on the 17th of August, 1849, a contract was come to between the East India Company of the one part and the East Indian Railway Company of the other part, in which the two agreed to co-operate in the construction "of a line of Railway from Calcutta towards the Upper Provinces," on certain conditions, the most important being :—

(1). That the East Indian Railway Company should pay into the Treasury of the East India Company, £1,000,000.

(2). That the East India Company should select the route and direction of a line of railway to be constructed as an experimental line ; such line to commence at Calcutta or within 10 miles of Calcutta, and to take such a direction as to form part of a line either to Mirzapore or to Rajmahal, at the option of the East India Company. Such selected line to be completed by the Railway Company, and opened for the conveyance of passengers and goods with all practicable speed.

(3). That the East India Company should provide the land required for the railway and for stations, offices and so forth.

(4). That the East Indian Railway Company should make such gradients, furnish rails of such weight and strength, and provide either single or double line as the East India Company would direct, and should also provide electric telegraphs and perform all such directions as might from time to time be given by the East India Company.

(5). That the Railway Company should provide a good and sufficient working stock and perform the duties of common carriers of goods and passengers, and allow the use of the railway to the public on terms to be approved by the East India Company, and charge such fares as should be approved by the East India Company.

(6). That the railway Company, its officers and servants, accounts and affairs be subject to the control and superintendence of the East India Company, and that all expenses be submitted for their sanction.

(7). That the Railway and its works be kept in a state of good repair to the satisfaction of the East India Company.

(8). That the East India Company pay the Railway Company interest at the rate of 5 per cent. per annum on the £1,000,000 paid to the East India Company, and that if the expenditure of the railway should exceed this sum, and further capital be raised, interest at the same rate be paid on it also.

(9). That the Railway Company convey the Government mails and post bags and servants of the post-office free of charge and convey troops and other Government officers and servants specified at reduced fares.

(10). That the railway become the property of the East India Company after 99 years, the engines, carriages, stock, machinery, and plant being paid for at a valuation.

The railway also had the right to surrender the line to the East India Company and the East India Company had a right of purchase on certain conditions, at any time within six months after the expiration of the first twenty-five years.

Such briefly were the terms of the first contract, and it seems unnecessary to detail the obstacles that had to be overcome before it was entered upon. For some years the Board were confronted with difficulties and opposed by persons whose interest seems to have been to prove that a railway, such as proposed, could not possibly pay. A Mr. John Bourne, for example, who had been a surveyor in the employment of the Company, advocated that a single line of railway laid upon the Grand Trunk road to Mirzapore, was all that was needed. and endeavoured to prove that a section of 150 miles out of Calcutta could not be profitable; he estimated the revenue on the traffic of the district between Calcutta and Burdwan, and putting this at a very low figure calculated that the working expenses, maintenance and depreciation would be so enormous that the outside dividend to be looked for would be under 2 per cent. on the capital. Mr. James Rendel disagreed entirely with Mr. Bourne's figures and estimated that even if his forecast of traffic was correct, a dividend of over 7 per cent. was far more probable. But this is only an instance of the criticism of the period. Others held that natives would not travel by railway, and that there was little need in a country like India which had river transport available, to construct a railroad for the movement of merchandise, which, they held, could not be carried by rail as cheaply as by river or road, while speed was no object. There were indeed many opponents to the scheme, but as the Board remarked at the time : " In the introduction of an undertaking so vast and distant there must always be difficulties in the first instance to surmount, but when the stake which the nation possesses in the interests of India, and the results likely to attend the introduction of railways into that country, are considered, the Board cannot doubt the disposition of all the authorities connected with the Government of India, to give those encouragements to the object, which are indispensable to induce capitalists to embark their money in it."

Among the most indefatigable workers on behalf of the Company was Mr. Stephenson, and that this was recognised at the time is apparent from a resolution of the shareholders recorded in 1849-1850 :—

"That in consideration of the services rendered by Mr. R. Macdonald Stephenson to this Company, and of the extraordinary exertions made, and the risks encountered by him, in introducing the railroad system into India, embracing three journeys to India and the survey of many hundred miles of railroad—it is the feeling of this meeting that he should be allowed a compensation for himself, and his family after his decease, by way of a percentage on the net profits, which, over and above 5 per cent. shall be received by the shareholders on the capital invested in the experimental section of railway now contemplated, and that the Directors be requested to take into consideration the rate of such percentage and submit the same to a future meeting of the proprietors."

The Directors subsequently recommended 5 per cent. as a suitable allowance, and Mr. Stephenson must have felt exceedingly satisfied. He embarked for India again in March 1850, together with Mr. George Turnbull, the Resident Engineer-in-Chief, and in less than a year the first section of the Company's proposed line was finally determined upon. "The Authorities," in the words of the Board, "have sanctioned the construction of a line of railroad from Howrah, opposite Calcutta, to Pundooah, with a branch line into the Raneegunge Collieries. The total length will be from 120 to 130 miles; and will in the first instance be laid with a single line of rails." At the same time contracts for the construction of the first 40 miles to Pundooah were let in India, and soon afterwards work was commenced, a gauge of five feet six inches being determined upon.

It is said that Lord Dalhousie actually decided the question of gauge for the first railway in India. At home there had been much controversy as to whether the gauge for English lines should be $4'8\frac{1}{2}''$ or $7'$.

Some railways were made to one, others to the other, Lord Dalhousie laid down that, in India, the gauge should be between these two extremes. Had it been possible for Lord Dalhousie to foresee subsequent developments he would probably have selected the 4' 8½" gauge, and if he had done so there would have been no excuse for introducing the complication of the metre gauge.

Mr. H. A. Aglionby, M.P., now became the Chairman of the Company, and during the early days of construction the reports of the Board were necessarily brief, but early in 1852, work having been started on the section between Pundooah and Raneegunge, it was decided that the main line to the North-West Provinces of India should proceed *via* Rajmahal, following the course of the Ganges, that is to say, by the route which forms what is now known as the loop line.

Early in 1854. the first section of the line to Raneegunge was completed, and Mr. Aglionby, addressing the shareholders, advised them that a new contract had been entered into with the East India Company to extend the railway to Delhi. Additional capital was now raised, and it was found that confidence in the prospects of the undertaking was gradually growing. As Mr. Aglionby remarked "it was the opinion of men best acquainted with mercantile matters that few, if any, companies in England at the present moment held out higher promise or better security than their own." Referring to the assistance given by the Company's Consulting Engineer he said : " he could not talk too highly of the indefatigable exertions and untiring energy of Mr. Rendel; the advanced state of the works would speak for themselves. Not only was the line from Calcutta to Raneegunge (a distance of 121 miles) almost finished, but an extended advance was actively going on to Rajmahal, a further increase of 120 miles," and it is interesting to record what Mr. Rendel said in reply. Mr. Rendel said, that the shareholders would be glad to learn that already forty-five miles of their line had been completed from Calcutta. There were engineering difficulties to contend with in India, which people at home could not possibly conceive. Yet he was bound to say that the works executed on their Indian lines were equal to any of the kind done in this country ; several large bridges had been built over nullahs and rivers near Hooghly, and on exceedingly treacherous, sinking and shifting ground. Yet no failures had happened nor had any accidents taken place, though since the planning of their railway, heavier floods had risen in Bengal than had been witnessed since the days of Clive. Before the end of the year the works would bring their rails to the Raneegunge coal fields and great profits would accrue when this was completed. On the opening of the line their rolling stock and engines would be found to equal anything of the sort in England. The Directors of the East India Company had readily met and concurred in all his suggestions and by the extraordinary exertions of their engineers, a survey to Allahabad had been taken in six months. Within four years their line would be advanced to this populous and important town, and seven years hence their railway would be running to Delhi.

From such speeches do we gain a glimpse of the work of construction in its earliest days, of the difficulties overcome and of the hopes for the future.

The first division of the experimental line from Howrah to Hooghly was opened for passenger traffic on the 15th August 1854, and a fortnight later an extension was opened to Pundooah. During the first sixteen weeks no less than 109,634 passengers were carried, and the gross earnings (including receipts for a few tons of merchandise) were £6,792 15s. 9d. or an average of £424 10s. 11$\frac{1}{8}$d. per week, and the Board reported that "looking to the small portion of line opened, the traffic has far exceeded the most sanguine expectations; and perhaps the most gratifying feature of all is in the fact that, contrary to a general belief in the indisposition and inability of the natives to avail themselves of railway communication, by far the largest number of passengers carried has been of the third class. The following is an analysis of the traffic:—First Class, 5,511; Second Class, 21,005; Third Class, 83,118."

It was considered a most extraordinary act that the very poorest of the inhabitants had availed themselves of the Railway directly it was opened. The third class fare was then ⅜d. per mile and there were only three classes, but the fact was proved that neither caste prejudices nor other considerations would prevent the native from making use of the new means of transport, though previous to this many, who should perhaps have been better informed, held a contrary opinion.

The line to Raneegunge was opened early in 1855, and this was held to be the termination of the first or experimental line. During the fifteen weeks after the line had been opened as far as Raneegunge, the number of passengers carried was 179,404 or an average of nearly 12,000 a week, and the earnings rose to about £900 a week.

Mr. R. W. Crawford, one of the Directors, who had been appointed Chairman of the Board of Directors, on the death of Mr. Aglionby, in his address to the Shareholders in August 1855, said that he looked upon the report on the traffic they had carried as most satisfactory " not only as regarded its amount and the prospect of its increase but also in this particular, that it put an end to the gloomy anticipations of those parties in this country, whose acquaintance with India was of a rather ancient date, and who were apprehensive that the prejudices of the natives would prevent them travelling by railway. Such was not the case." Mr. Crawford added that he had been himself in India and knew that the natives were fully alive to everything that could improve their position. They were aware that time was to them, as to the people of Europe, a great element of profit, and they would, therefore, avail themselves of a means of speedy transit from place to place, in preference to exercising the natural means of locomotion.

It may here be remarked that prolonged experience has shewn that no truer words were ever spoken. The native of India likes to travel as fast as he can be carried, and at the present time there is no better proof of this than the preference given to the recently-introduced third class express trains over the slow passenger trains, but it took many years to recognise this, and it was not until 1897, during the Chairmanship of General Sir Richard Strachey, that third class passengers were first admitted to the mail trains below Allahabad, and not until 1905 that express trains were first run for lower class passengers.

CHAPTER II.

PROGRESS OF CONSTRUCTION. EFFECT OF THE MUTINY. VISIT OF MR. A. M. RENDEL TO INDIA.

WE have seen that the first contract with the East India Company was dated the 17th August 1849, that Mr. Stephenson proceeded to India shortly afterwards, and in conjunction with the Government Engineers, decided upon the route the experimental line should follow, and that in 1854, or within three and-a-half years of the time in which the land necessary for the purpose had been made over, the Railway was opened as far as Hooghly, and shortly afterwards as far as Raneegunge. Considering that all the permanent-way, rolling-stock and other stores had to be transported from England, in sailing ships viâ the Cape, the time taken was by no means long. By 1856, contracts had been entered upon for all the rails that would be required to construct the line from Calcutta to Delhi, a distance of about 1,000 miles. That is to say a line which would be about as long as from Land's End to the North of Scotland and back again.

During the eleven months of 1855, in which the line was open from Calcutta to Raneegunge, no fewer than 617,281 passengers were carried, an amount of traffic quite sufficient to satisfy the most sceptical of the travelling propensities of the natives of India, and beyond this there was an immediate development of the goods traffic. Contracts were entered upon to carry over 100,000 tons of coal from Raneegunge to Calcutta, and a quantity of ordinary merchandise was transported, which, though comparatively small, gave hope for the future. In the second half of 1855, the revenue from coaching traffic was £25,000, from goods traffic £6,385, from coal £7,856, and the working expenses amounted to 42 per cent. of the gross traffic receipts. During 1856 the traffic continued to develop, and the working expenses were considerably reduced. In this year Mr. Stephenson's health failed, and he was compelled to relinquish his duties as Agent of the Company in India, to be succeeded in 1857 by Mr. Edward Palmer who had had a training on the Great Western and Great Northern Railways of England. Mr. Stephenson now joined the Board of Directors in London.

The Company's Consulting Engineer, Mr. James Meadows Rendel, who had rendered most valuable service to the Company, and had always expressed the greatest faith in its prospects, died in 1857 and was succeeded by his sons, Messrs. A. M. and G. Rendel, but the latter shortly afterwards joined the firm of Messrs. Armstrong, leaving the work of the East Indian Railway entirely in the hands of Mr. A. M. (now Sir Alexander) Rendel, who has continued to be the Company's Consulting Engineer ever since. Proposals were under consideration at this time for two most important extensions of the Railway, the first from Mirzapore to Jubbulpore to connect with the Great Indian Peninsula Railway running from Bombay, the second from Delhi to Lahore.

In the spring of 1857 it was that the Great Mutiny broke out, and, as a consequence, a large portion of the work of construction was delayed, while all new projects had to stand over.

The Board's report to the shareholders dated the 29th of October 1857, gives some account of the Company's affairs in that memorable year, and the following extract from it will be read with interest:

"The unfortunate events occurring in India at the present time have, doubtless, created some anxiety as to the effect which they may have had on the progress of the Company's operations, and the Board avail themselves of this opportunity of making the Proprietors acquainted with the circumstances of the Company to the latest date They beg to report that, whilst in common with the rest of the community, the Company has suffered by the mutiny, it has not sustained that serious amount of damage which might have been feared; as, irrespective of the sacrifice of valuable lives, which the Board most deeply lament, the chief loss it will have to deplore will be that arising from the temporary stoppage of the principal portion of the works and the consequent delay in their completion. In the Lower Provinces, for instance, the damage done to the Company's property has been mainly confined, as far as the Board is aware, to certain station works, and the preparations made for the Soane bridge; and in the Upper Provinces and on the River to the destruction of some of its buildings, machinery and tools. It has been a source of sincere gratification to the Board to observe the praiseworthy efforts which have been made by the members of the Staff to protect the Company's property, surrounded as in many cases they have been with great personal dangers. It would be invidious, where all have conducted themselves so well, to particularize individuals, but the Board cannot refrain from noticing in terms of the highest commendation the conduct of Messrs. Boyle and Kelly in the gallant defence at Arrah, and in doing so they are satisfied that they only echo the feelings of the entire executive in India."

The "gallant defence at Arrah" was one of the most glorious episodes of the mutiny, and the name of Vicars Boyle, the East Indian Railway engineer who rendered the defence possible, will ever be remembered, recorded as it is in every history of the great struggle. It need only be said here that among his colleagues he was always afterwards known as "Victor Boyle."

Although the mutiny retarded the work of construction, the traffic on such portions of the line as were already opened for traffic continued to develop, and there was a very great growth in the revenue, the total receipts for the year 1857 being £132,434 2s. 11d. against £96,100 10s. 2d. in 1856.

In 1858 the terms for constructing the branch to Jubbulpore were concluded, and were, generally speaking, precisely the same as for the remainder of the line. Interest on the additional capital required was guaranteed by Government at 5 per cent. per annum, and it was stipulated that the accounts were to be kept altogether distinct from those pertaining to the line to Delhi.

During 1858 considerable progress was made, and the line between Allahabad and Cawnpore was completed. In this year also Mr. Meadows Rendel sailed for Calcutta in order to have an opportunity of becoming personally acquainted with the local conditions of the country. Mr. Rendel returned to England before the close of the year, having inspected the works along the entire length of the Railway as far as Cawnpore, beyond which it was not safe to proceed, and the Board had every reason to be satisfied with the result of his journey. Among other matters dealt with by him, a very considerable saving was effected by his decision to introduce iron girders instead of brick arches in the construction of bridges, while a difficulty which had arisen in the transport up-country of materials, stores and rolling-stock was overcome, at his suggestion, by building light-draught steamers and flats for the transport service of the Company. Some of these vessels were built in England and some in Calcutta, and a means of relief afforded which could not otherwise have been effected.

We must now go back a few years to give a brief account of a project which will be referred to again elsewhere but should also be mentioned here. In 1856 the Board of Directors, hearing that a plan for constructing a bridge over the river Hooghly was under consideration, and that a new Port subsidiary to Calcutta, was about to be established on the river Mutlah, offered to make the surveys of a line of railway to connect that Port with the Company's line.

The Court of Directors of the East India Company, having considered the matter, took the view that it was then premature to connect Mutlah with Calcutta by railway, and told the Board so.

In the meantime, however, another Company was established for the express purpose of making this railway, and proposed to raise the necessary capital without any guarantee of interest. On this the Secretary of State for India invited the Board to express their views. They replied in these terms "in the present state of the question of bridging the Hooghly, they are not prepared to recommend the Proprietors to undertake the construction of the Railway in question, but if any concession for the line should be made to third parties, it is their conviction that a clause should be inserted, requiring the sale of the line to the East Indian Railway Company hereafter, on terms to be settled by arbitration, should the public interests render such a course desirable," and so the question of directly connecting the East Indian Railway with a subsidiary port to Calcutta on the river Mutlah remained in abeyance until it was re-opened by Col. Gardiner, Agent of the Company, many years afterwards.

At this time it had been proposed to entrust the construction of an extension of the Railway from Delhi to Lahore to the East Indian Railway Company, and surveys were taken by the Company's Officers of the river Sutlej, with a view to determining the best point at which that river should be crossed, but in 1859, the Government decided to make this section over to another Company, then known as the "Punjab Railway" and the Board relinquished their claim.

In the meantime the survey of the Jubbulpore branch was being pushed on, and it may here be mentioned that, while in the prosecution of this work, Mr. Evans, the Chief Engineer, and Mr. Limnell, his Assistant, were attacked and murdered by a party of rebels. Mr. Limnell "whose qualifications," in the words of the Board, "were reported to be of the highest order, had but lately joined the service, but Mr. Evans was one of the oldest and most respected of the Company's officers, and had only recently been promoted to the post which he held at the time of his death."

Some details of this incident taken from an account given me by Mr. H. Wenden, C.I.E., now Agent of the Great Indian Peninsular Railway, but at the time a young engineer on construction work, supplemented by an account by Mr. John Lewis, who was an engineer on the Jubbulpore line shortly after the occurrence, are of considerable interest.

During the cold season of 1858-9 Mr. Evans, Chief Engineer of the Allahabad-Jubbulpore extension survey party, together with Messrs. Limnell and Colin Campbell, two of his assistants, were in camp in Rewah territory at a place called Entowah. They had just finished their midday meal when Campbell hearing a "bobbery" looked out of his tent and saw a *posse* of armed natives bearing down on the camp. His *sais*, an old grey-bearded Mahomedan, ran up to Colin Campbell with his grey horse saddled and got him on to it. By hard riding he managed to reach Manickpore in safety, though chased for many miles by *sowars*, and the next day went on to Allahabad where he reported the tragedy.

Mr. John Lewis says, " Colin Campbell took me over the route of his escape, and how he stuck on his horse over such a country is one of the marvels of horsemanship."

The men who made the attack on the camp were part of a band of outlaws cast off from Tantia Topee's force and led by a mutineer named Runmust Singh, who, after Evans' head had been cut off, ordered Limnell to carry it.

Limnell carried it until he was exhausted and then Runmust Singh ordered some of his men to kill him; this they refused to do saying they had killed one *sahib*, he must kill the other, which he did by shooting him down.

The country was scoured by a body of Alexander's Horse and some Gurkhas, and shortly afterwards Runmust Singh was captured and hanged in Rewah.

Throughout 1859, construction proceeded apace, work progressed along several sections of the Railway simultaneously. The chief difficulty lay in the transport of material up country, and another trouble of a more temporary nature was a terrible cholera epidemic which ravaged the Rajmahal District during October and November of that year. For some weeks no less than eight to ten per cent. of the coolies employed died weekly, and the disease did not altogether disappear until the middle of December. During the epidemic it is estimated that over 4,000 labourers succumbed, and the reports of the engineers engaged on construction shew what a trying time they had.

But by the close of 1859, considerable progress had been made. The 24 miles between the river Adjai and Sainthea station, the remaining portion of the South Beerbhoom District, had been opened for traffic, while the section to Rajmahal was almost completed. From Rajmahal also, as far as Colgong, the works were in a forward state, and good progress was being made with sections beyond as far as Monghyr, the Jamalpur tunnel was in course of construction, and the only bar to progress further north was the want of bridge and permanent way material which could not be forwarded sufficiently quickly.

In the North-West Provinces also work was already going on as far as Agra, while arrangements were in progress for getting possession of the necessary land for the entrance into Delhi. The Board reported that "the great difficulty still to be overcome is the transport of permanent-way materials from Calcutta to the works", but they had every confidence that "when the line is opened to Rajmahal, and their steam flotilla is fairly at work, this last remaining bar to completion will be removed."

Let us now glance at the traffic being carried in these early days.

During the year 1859, the number of passengers carried was 1,388,714 against 1,172,852 in the previous year.

The weight of goods carried was 299,424 tons against 190,566 tons in 1858, and the increase in the mineral traffic was so great that it was decided to extend what was then known as the branch to the collieries, from Raneegunge to Barrakur.

The net traffic receipts, converted into pounds sterling at the rate of 2s. the rupee, are shewn in the following table:—

Year	Miles	£	s.	d.
1855		31,252	12	9
1856	121 miles.	57,060	1	6
1857		82,770	11	6
1858	142 ,,	88,148	2	10
1859	166 ,,	128,534	8	6

In 1855, the net receipts per mile open per week were £4 19s. 4d., in 1859, £16 9s. 7d. The percentage of working expenses to receipts were, in 1855, 53·26, in 1859, 44·85. The number of passengers and tons of goods carried compared :—

1855.		1859.	
Passengers.	Goods.	Passengers.	Goods.
No.	Tons.	No.	Tons.
790,281	27,213	1,388,714	299,424.

At the end of 1859, there were 19 passenger and 30 goods engines running on the line, and 8 passenger and 20 goods engines under construction or repair, the whole of the coaching stock amounted to 228 vehicles, while the goods stock only totalled 848 wagons.

CHAPTER III.

OPENING OF THE RAILWAY TO RAJMAHAL AND SUBSEQUENTLY TO DELHI.—RETIREMENT OF MR GEORGE TURNBULL, THE FIRST RAILWAY ENGINEER IN INDIA.—THE CONSTRUCTION OF THE CHORD LINE DECIDED UPON.—UNEXPECTED GROWTH OF TRAFFIC, FOLLOWED BY COMPLAINTS OF WANT OF ADEQUATE FACILITIES.

ON the 4th July 1860, the first train ran through from Calcutta to Rajmahal, and on the 15th October following this section of the Railway was advertised as open to the public, the interval of the rains having been employed in putting the line into efficient order, and allowing the earthwork to settle and consolidate. "Great expectations," the Board said, "have been formed of the large traffic which will come upon this portion of the line, but the Board think it right to guard the shareholders against too sanguine an expectation that this traffic will appear simultaneously with its opening. It will certainly take time to draw it from its accustomed channels, and whilst no doubt there will at once be a very considerable apparent tonnage conveyed, it will principally be in the Company's own materials, the real trade of the country coming gradually, and until the advantages of railway transit are better understood in India, probably in the first instance somewhat slowly."

To commemorate the opening of the line as far as Rajmahal, the Government of India struck a large silver medal which was distributed to the principal officers engaged on the work. The following is a copy of the communication sent to one of the District Engineers employed on the work :—

FROM
>THE SECRETARY TO GOVT. OF INDIA.
>*Public Works Department.*

To
>GRAHAM PEDDIE, ESQ.,
>>DISTRICT ENGINEER,
>>>*East Indian Railway.*

SIR,

I AM commanded by His Excellency the Viceroy and Governor-General of India to transmit, for your acceptance, the medal struck by order of Government on the occasion of opening the East Indian Railway to the Ganges at Rajmahal, as being a memorable point attained in the construction of that great work, on which you have been employed.

>I have the honour to be
>>SIR,
>>>Your most obedient servant,
>>>>H. YULE, LIEUT.-COL.,
>>>>>*Secretary to the Govt. of India.*

The Company had now 249 miles at work in Bengal and 126 miles open for traffic in the North-West Provinces, and during the year 1860 the additional length of 87 miles from Cawnpore to Etawah, was opened to traffic. Certain considerations, however, rendered it desirable to postpone the construction of the Jubbulpore section and this part of the scheme was, for the time being, placed in abeyance.

During 1861, further sections of the line were opened for traffic, $72\frac{1}{2}$ miles in Bengal and $120\frac{3}{4}$ miles in the North-West Provinces, and by the beginning of 1862 the line was completed to Monghyr, so that the Company had at work $359\frac{1}{2}$ miles in Bengal and $243\frac{3}{4}$ miles in the North-West Provinces, or a total of $603\frac{1}{4}$ miles, and there was every hope that the whole of the main line would be completed by the end of 1862. In this year also it was determined to proceed with the construction of the Jubbulpore branch.

Throughout 1863 various sections of the main line were completed, but it was not until the 1st August, 1864, that the East Indian Railway was opened up to the banks of the river Jumna at Delhi. The delay was largely due to a question having been raised by Government as to the route the line should follow. In the words of the Board " The large bridge over the Jumna at Delhi was being rapidly pushed forward when the Government of India proposed that the line should proceed to Lahore, *viâ* Meerut and Saharanpur, instead of from Delhi, in a direct line to Ferozepore. Pending the settlement of this question, the principal works on this bridge have been temporarily suspended, because the arrangement now suggested might render it desirable to complete the bridge as a road bridge into Delhi instead of as a railway bridge. This alteration is undoubtedly of great advantage to the Company engaged on the Lahore line, and appears to have been originated by the Government for good and sufficient reasons; but it has necessarily involved many serious considerations, which the Directors of this Company have, on public grounds, and in the interests of this Company, thought it right to submit to the Secretary of State."

The question was discussed at great length, but in the end the problem was solved by a compromise. It was agreed that the East Indian Railway should run into Delhi, and that the Punjab line should be constructed *viâ* Meerut and Saharanpur but that it should also have access to Delhi by running over a short section (12 miles) of the East Indian Railway from Ghaziabad. Mr. Crawford, Chairman of the Board, in his address to the shareholders in April 1864 said that "It was a great gratification to him to state that the line from Calcutta to Delhi was open for traffic with the exception of the bridge over the Jumna at Allahabad. They could now take passengers over their line from Calcutta to Delhi and *vice versâ* a distance of 1,020 miles. He thought everyone must admit that notwithstanding the various difficulties and obstructions thrown in their way from time to time, the progress they had made was very satisfactory. They could not compare the work on any line in England, either for magnitude or length of continuous line, with their East Indian line. There was not a line on any part of the Continent to compare with it. Even the Grand Trunk line of Canada could not compare with it as to works, progress or length of line. The completion of the works at the Delhi end of the line had been impeded by considerations as to route and in respect of the point of junction with the Punjab line. The original course of the line had been altered by the Government and it was now to go, through the centre of the Doab between two rivers, in the direction of Delhi. The Punjab line had also been altered so that both lines should enter Delhi. These alterations in route had caused great delay in finishing the third great bridge, involving considerable expense to the Company. The works on the Jubbulpore line were proceeding satisfactorily, and there was every reason to believe that the line would be completed by 1866. From information they had received, there was no doubt the works would be completed on the Jubbulpore line to its junction with the Bombay Railway at Jubbulpore and be ready for exchanging traffic with the Great Indian Peninsula Company when they could meet them with their line."

At this period the construction of the present main or Chord Line was already under consideration, several alternative routes had

MEDAL STRUCK IN COMMEMORATION OF THE OPENING OF THE RAILWAY TO RAJMAHAL.

"Prosper thou the work of our hands upon us : O Prosper thou our handy-work.—Ps. XC."

The East Indian Railway projected by Rowland Macdonald Stephenson, George Turnbull being Chief Engineer, was commenced in the XVth year of the reign of Victoria : James Andrew, Marquis of Dalhousie, K.T., being Governor General of India ; and was opened to Rajmahal in the XXIVth year of the same gracious reign : Charles John Earl Canning, G.C.B., being Viceroy and Governor-General, A.D., MDCCCLX.

been surveyed and Government was being pressed to sanction the adoption of one of them. The great advantage of the Chord line was that it would shorten the distance for carrying "through traffic" by nearly 100 miles and save the expense of doubling the circuitous route viâ the Loop or then Main line.

In the meanwhile, the Government was full of appreciation of the results already attained. On the 25th August, 1863, the Secretary to the Government of Bengal, Railway Branch, wrote to the Secretary to the Government of India :—

"With reference to the results shewn in the Revenue Account of the East Indian Railway for the last half year, which have been prominently noticed in the note submitted to the Government of India, I am instructed to state that the Lieutenant-Governor desires to express the gratification with which he regards the successful issue of the operations of the season. The vast amount of traffic, both in passengers and goods, which has been attracted to the Railway during the first six months of its opening to Benares, notwithstanding the novelty of the undertaking, the necessarily imperfect nature of the station accommodation, the inexperience of the establishments and the insufficient available means, both of locomotion and transport, reflects, in His Honor's opinion, the highest credit on the Company's officers, especially those of the Traffic Department, with Mr. Batchelor at their head, and holds out an almost certain promise that the Railway in a short time will not only become independent of the guarantee and yield a profit in excess of 5 per cent. to the shareholders, but may conduce beyond all former expectation to the wealth and improvement of the country, and to the strength and financial prosperity of the Government."

Previous to this the Viceroy, Lord Elgin, had personally gone over the line from Calcutta to Benares, and we must not omit to notice the following extract from the official Gazette, in which is recorded what he observed on his journey, and his appreciation of the work done by the Company's Chief Engineer in Bengal, Mr. George Turnbull, who, after thirteen years laborious duty, found that his health would no longer permit him to give the Company the benefit of his services, and was about to leave India. The Board, in referring to the acknowledgment by Government of Mr. Turnbull's unique services, remarked that :—

"Gratifying as any such tokens of respect would doubtless be to Mr. Turnbull, they will be nothing as compared with the reward he will find in the contemplation of the kindly feelings with which future ages of India will unquestionably regard the name of the man whose genius planned and whose indomitable courage and perseverance have carried out the magnificent series of works entrusted to his care."

Extract from "Official Gazette."

Benares, February 7th, 1863.—H. E. the Viceroy on his arrival at this city desires to congratulate the officers of the East Indian Railway Company and the public on the completion of the additional section of the Grand Trunk line of Railway, from Calcutta to the North-West Provinces, that has been recently opened to Benares, and on the prospects of the early opening of the whole line for traffic up to Allahabad and Delhi.

2. The distance from Calcutta by rail to Benares is 541 miles. Work was begun in 1851. The line to Burdwan was opened in February 1855; to Adjai in October 1858; to Rajmahal in October 1859; to Bhagulpore in 1861; to Monghyr in February 1862, and to opposite Benares in December 1862. In ten years therefore have been opened (including branches) a continuous length of 601 miles, being at the rate of 60 miles a year. This is exclusive of the portion of the line already finished between Allahabad and Agra in the North-West Provinces, and of the sections from Agra and Allyghur, which it is expected will be ready in a few weeks. Including this length, the progress of the East Indian Railway has not been short of ninety

miles a year—a rate which, if it has not come up to the expectations first entertained is, under all the circumstances of the case, satisfactory as regards the past and encouraging as regards the future.

3. On his journey from Calcutta to Benares H. E. observed, with much interest, the numerous striking works that have been so successfully constructed on this Railway by the Company's engineers, and viewed with particular admiration the great girder bridge over the Soane, which, it is believed, is exceeded in magnitude by only one bridge in the world. The smaller girder bridges over the Kiul and Hullohur, the heavy flood arching in the vicinity of these rivers, the masonry bridges over the Adjai and More and the Monghyr tunnel, also attracted the attention of H. E. the Viceroy, as works of more than ordinary difficulty designed and carried out with signal ability.

4. H. E. the Governor-General gladly accepts this opportunity of acknowledging the services rendered by the officers of the Railway Company in the prosecution of this great work; and of expressing more specially the strong sense he entertains of the high engineering skill and the steady devotion to his duties exhibited by Mr. George Turnbull, the Chief Engineer of the Company in Bengal, who, in a few days, will give up the direction of the works which he has now seen completed. Although not in the immediate employment of the Government, Mr. Turnbull has, in the opinion of H. E., well earned the expression of the thanks of the Governor-General for his professional services. which have, indeed, been rendered as much to the public as to the Railway Company. In all Mr. Turnbull's dealings with the officers of the Government, he has invariably shewn that moderation and desire to conciliate, which were essential for the harmonious and successful carrying on of the railway works, under the peculiar conditions imposed by the terms of the Government guarantee; and the Governor-General has much satisfaction in signifying, on behalf of the Government of India, his high estimation of the manner in which all Mr. Turnbull's relations with the Government have been conducted.

5. H. E. the Viceroy will not fail to bring to the favourable notice of H. M.'s Government the long and excellent services of Mr. Turnbull, who, having been the first Railway Engineer employed in India, has now happily seen the portion of this great work on which he was more particularly engaged brought to a close, after many years of arduous and persevering labour, under circumstances of unusual difficulty,

with the most complete satisfaction to his employers and to the Government, and with the highest credit to himself.

(SD.) R. STRACHEY, LIEUT.-COL., R.E.,
Secretary to the Government of India with the Governor-General.

Mr. Turnbull had encountered and overcome various difficulties. Besides the magnitude of the works, the construction of a railway was a novelty in India and a practical knowledge of the country, the people, and their language had to be acquired. The native had to be trained to accomplish tasks entirely foreign to anything he had seen or heard of before and the wonderful adaptability which enabled him to carry out, under European guidance, the construction of a railroad was in itself an indication that he would afterwards be able to take charge of its stations and goods sheds, maintain its permanent way and buildings, construct its engines and rolling stock, work its telegraph and carry out, often under the most trying circumstances and contending against all manner of difficulties, every kind of duty that would be likely to be required of him.

In the early progress of the work the engineers were much impeded by the Sonthal insurrection, and the importation of labourers from Nagpur and other distant parts became a necessity. The unhealthiness of some parts of the country, especially about the base of the Rajmahal hills, was the cause of great delays, while from Monghyr upwards the effect of the Indian Mutiny was to throw back progress for nearly two years. The circumstances of the route having been taken along the banks of the Hooghly, the Bhagarathi and the Ganges made it necessary to cross all the affluents of those great rivers, involving large bridges and extensive viaducts, besides embankments of unusual length and size, and if any pioneer of railway construction deserves a memorial to his name it is Mr. George Turnbull.

Mr. Turnbull was succeeded by Mr. Samuel Power who had been Superintending Engineer of the Soane bridge. At this time the line had three Chief Engineers; Mr. Turnbull had been Chief Engineer of the Bengal Division, Mr. George Sibley was Chief Engineer of the North-West Provinces, and Mr. Henry P. Le Mesurier was Chief Engineer of the Jubbulpore line. On the opening of the line to Delhi Mr. Sibley also received the thanks of Government.

By 1864 the traffic of the East Indian Railway had fast outgrown the facilities for dealing with it; stock could not be constructed fast enough to carry the traffic but, as the Board explained, "there was no blame for deficiency in rolling stock or other matters that could be laid to the Board. They had sent out a large quantity of material, including ironwork for carriages and wagons; but the workshops and factories had been unable to supply the carriages fast enough." It is curious to read now of stock difficulties so far back as 1864; the same cry had been heard ten years before then and has continued to the present time. But it was not only in regard to shortage of wagons that there was, even in those early days, difficulty in dealing with the traffic offering. Then, as now, the terminal facilities were totally inadequate. In his report for the first half of 1864 Mr. Power, Chief Engineer, Bengal Division, remarks :—

"It is to be regretted that no improvement has taken place in the terminus at Howrah, where, at this season, it is distressing to witness the general embarrassment of the traffic and the destruction of cotton, grain and other property, arising principally from the want of accommodation at this station, from whence confusion appears to be propagated over all the line. * * * The heavy expenditure on permanent goods sheds, formerly proposed, would not be expedient now, when the establishment of a great metropolitan station in Calcutta is under discussion,"

While the Board said :—

"At present the terminus of the line was at Howrah opposite Calcutta, but everybody said the proper place for the terminus was in Calcutta itself, and it was proposed that the East Indian line should be brought across the Hooghly, by a bridge at a point about two miles above Calcutta, and thus be brought into the city itself, and there form junctions with two other Railways. The capital required for this purpose was about £1,000,000."

The question of bridging the Hooghly and constructing a terminus in Calcutta was jointly considered by Mr. A. M. Rendel, the Company's Consulting Engineer, and Mr. Power, who in 1865 reported as follows :—

"It can hardly be expected that the community of Calcutta should be contented with their present means of access to the Railway, and it has long been foreseen that as soon as the value of railway communication in India was established, a demand would be made for a more perfect connection with the capital. As far back as 1854, the subject was referred by the then Government of India to the late Mr. Rendel. During the Mutiny, and for a few years subsequent to it, the attention of the public was otherwise occupied, but early in 1862 Mr. Turnbull, by the direction of the Government, prepared plans for a bridge over the Hooghly, near Pultah Ghât. In the early part of last year the Eastern Bengal Railway Company proposed to connect their line with the East Indian by a bridge 30 miles above Calcutta. This scheme would have had the effect of transferring to the Eastern Bengal the whole of the East Indian through traffic for the same length. It was therefore opposed by the Board and ultimately rejected by the Government of India, apparently on the ground that, in the interest of the public, the bridge should be placed as near as possible to Calcutta, and should be a part of the East Indian Railway system. Finally, towards the close of last year, a Committee was appointed in India by the Governor-General to investigate the question in connection with the improvement of the port generally. The Board are in possession of the evidence taken before the Committee and the report which they have had based upon it. It is sufficient here to say that we fully agree with the Committee in regard to the necessity for the bridge and terminal station in Calcutta, also in regard to the site selected for them. We have reason also to believe that the Government of India entertain a similar opinion; and however much the Board may desire to avoid so important an increase of the Company's responsibilities, yet if it is offered to them under the usual guarantee, they cannot, in our opinion, if they would be uncontrolled in the use of their access to Calcutta, refuse to undertake it."

Further reference will be made to this proposal of bridging the Hooghly and constructing in Calcutta a central station. Suffice to say for the present that we know what has actually been done. The Hooghly has not been bridged in the immediate vicinity of the city, except by a floating roadway and there is no central station. The East Indian Railway crosses the river about 25 miles North of Calcutta and runs on the metals of the Eastern Bengal Railway to the Kidderpore Docks, on the southern outskirts of the city, and the idea of bridging the Hooghly and constructing a central station is apparently further off accomplishment than it was in 1864.

Other schemes for improving facilities of transport were however being also considered and notably the construction of the chord line from Raneegunge to Luckieserai on the Ganges. This scheme was strongly supported by Mr. Rendel on the ground that it would save doubling the Loop line between Khana and Luckieserai, a distance of 252 miles, it would have the effect of bringing the coalfields 200 miles nearer the centre of the Company's system, thus benefiting not only the Company but the public, and it would greatly shorten the distance between Calcutta and the North-West Provinces, the more material point being that it would place Allahabad, where the traffic of the North-West Provinces would diverge to the east or west, in a position that would go far to counterbalance the advantage which Bombay has been assumed to possess over Calcutta as a shipping port.

The arguments in favour of the chord line were such as could not be controverted and the scheme was carried. I do not think that at the present day any better arguments could be advanced in favour of the grand chord line now under construction. The position at the time was that the single line *viâ* the loop could not carry the traffic offering, in fact it was the general opinion that it could not carry sufficient traffic to earn more than a net revenue of 5 per cent. Therefore the question to decide was whether this single line, traversing a round about route should be doubled, or whether a new line by a shorter route should be constructed. The decision was in favour of the shorter route, but in the meantime considerable pressure was put upon the Secretary of State and the Board to double the loop or old line, as well as to construct the new route *viâ* the chord. The Government of India and the Bengal Chamber of Commerce both urged upon the Secretary of State the necessity for this being done, but the Board shared the opinion of their chief engineer, Mr. Power, that such a course was quite unnecessary and eventually the Secretary of State accepted the views of the Board. That these views were correct is proved by the fact that up to the present time the loop line remains single and fully meets traffic requirements.

The work of constructing the chord line was exceedingly slow and it was not opened for public traffic until the 1st January 1871, although the centre line had been set out by the engineers early in 1865. It is true that the country is broken and difficult and that the thick jungle necessitated very close examination to select the best ground, but after all this had been done there were great difficulties with the contractors who had taken up the work of construction and it was on this account that the chief delay occurred.

The bridge over the Jumna at Allahabad was opened for traffic on the 15th August, 1865. It had taken nearly 8 years to construct and its completion was a subject for much congratulation; it was the middle link in the long chain of unbroken communication established by the East Indian Railway, for the first time in the history of India, between the right bank of the Hooghly at Calcutta and the left bank of the Jumna at Delhi. Mr. Sibley, the Chief Engineer of the North-West Provinces and Messrs. Collett and Donne, the District and Assistant Engineers and the subordinate staff under them received the thanks of Government and the encomiums of the Board.

The only remaining works of construction now in hand were the bridge across the Jumna at Delhi together with the station arrangements in that city, the Jubbulpore branch and the chord line with its branch to the Giridih collieries. It was also decided to double part of the line, which was then all single with the exception of the Burdwan-Howrah section.

The Jumna bridge at Delhi was opened for traffic in 1866, this was the last of the great bridges and its completion meant in the words of Mr. Crawford, the Chairman of the Board, that "a passenger starting from Calcutta could cross the river in one of the Company's ferry boats to their present terminus at Howrah and from thence, by one of the Company's trains proceed to the city of Delhi in the same carriage over the whole distance."

The Jubbulpore branch was not completed and opened for traffic before the 1st June, 1867, but prior to this date a temporary coach service was established between Jubbulpore and Nagpur, the then terminus of the Great Indian Peninsular Railway, so that passengers were able to proceed from Calcutta to Bombay and *vice versâ*, the journey from Calcutta occupying about five days and the cost being Rs. 231-2-6. Rather different to the ordinary first class fare of Rs. 91-11-0 now in force.

A word as to the growth of traffic is now desirable. For the first time in the history of the undertaking, the net earnings during the half year ended the 30th June, 1866, enabled a dividend to be declared, exceeding the guaranteed interest of 5 per cent., the additional dividend was at the rate of $\frac{1}{2}$ per cent. and so within 12 years of the opening of its first section, the corner was turned in which the Railway began to earn something beyond what the Goverment had guaranteed to the shareholders.

In a previous chapter the annual net earnings were given to the end of 1859, and continuing this we find them to have been during the next seven years :—

		£	s.	d.
1860	... ...	211,680	14	10
1861	... ...	263,025	1	9
1862	... ...	269,406	10	5
1863	... ...	439,964	9	3
1864	... ...	625,894	12	4
1865	... ...	928,751	1	11
1866	... ...	1,119,315	6	2

In 1859, under a million and a half passengers were carried, in 1886 the number had risen to considerably over four millions, while the weight of goods and minerals lifted had, in the same period, risen from 299,424 to 802,043 tons. In the working expenses however there was very little improvement; standing at 44·85 per cent. of the gross earnings in 1859 they had only been reduced to 44·34 per cent. in 1866.

The growth of traffic had, as previously indicated, been far beyond the most sanguine expectations and considerable dissatisfaction was expressed by the public at the inadequate facilities provided by the Railway. In his address to the shareholders on the 29th June, 1866, Mr. Crawford referred at some length to the complaints made. He said :—

"The subject of traffic naturally suggests to me the complaints which have been made in India during the last four months with respect to the management of our line. And

COMPLAINTS OF INADEQUATE FACILITIES. 45

upon that I must say that while, undoubtedly, a single line has not been found equal to the conveyance of the traffic of that part of India which it serves, so efficiently as we should desire, still I am bound to say that I cannot accept on the part of the Company any blame in consequence. It was not at all unreasonable to expect that when the line was completed throughout, the traffic of that part of India would be brought on our line, in a great degree deserting the old modes of conveyance, whether by road or by river. But it would have been, I apprehend, an unwise policy on our part to have anticipated that event to the fullest extent, even if we had the means to do so, because if any disappointment had ensued, then I think, the Directors would have been fairly chargeable with something approaching to rashness if they had embarked your money in an unnecessary outlay."

Such was the explanation of the Chairman of the Directors, and from it, if from nothing else, the fact clearly stands out that the traffic to be carried far exceeded all anticipations. The Railway in short was quite unprepared for the demands made upon it, but considering the expenditure that improvements of facilities would have involved, caution was needed and the Directors could not be blamed for exercising caution or for taking time to consider and examine what was best to be done. The merchants of Calcutta held a meeting at which some resolutions were passed, first "That no check of any kind should be placed on the supply of rolling stock till the requirements of the traffic are satisfied." Secondly "That the line should be doubled throughout its entire length with as little delay as possible." Thirdly "That by means of a bridge over the Hooghly at Calcutta, the terminus of the line should be transferred from Howrah to the metropolis, and if possible, to some central position which shall form a terminus common to all lines entering this City."

Now it would have cost probably six millions sterling to double the line throughout and to add such a supply of stock as would meet all the requirements of the busiest season and the interests of the shareholders had to be considered—but apart from this it would not have been possible at the time to raise in London so large an amount of additional capital. Therefore the Board had to add to the facilities by degrees. Over 99 per cent. of the capital of the East Indian Railway had been subscribed in London and the Chairman held the opinion that it was not quite reasonable that merchants in India should expect other people to find an unlimited amount for the purpose of enabling the Railway, upon an emergency, to meet every possible demand made upon it. "But," he added, "with a great traffic existing, with the certainty before us that the traffic when fully developed will be sufficient to pay a very large return, even as a double line, I have no doubt whatever, that our policy of gradually doubling the line at convenient places, from time to time, and as gradually stocking it, will answer all the just expectations that can be entertained of us."

At this time the line was about to be doubled from Luckieserai, where the Chord

ADDITIONS TO ROLLING STOCK.

and Loop lines met, as far as Allahabad and arrangements had been made for the supply of no less than 215 additional locomotives. In addition to this the rolling stock was being materially added to, so that the Board of Directors were doing all that could well be expected of them and were by no means asleep to the position.

CHAPTER IV.

THE ALIGNMENT OF THE EAST INDIAN RAILWAY AND OTHER MATTERS.

THE actual route the East Indian Railway should follow on its course from Calcutta to Delhi, naturally formed a subject for much controversy. The general idea was to get to Delhi through Mirzapore and the original survey was made with the intention of taking the line very much along the course of the route now being constructed as the Grand Chord; it was in fact at first proposed to run the lower section of the railroad in as direct a line as possible to Benares.

Had this idea been adopted, the selection would not have been without distinct advantages. It would, in the first place, have given a far shorter route to the North-West Provinces than that afforded by the Loop line; secondly it would have led to the discovery of the Jherriah Coalfield forty years earlier than it was actually opened up; and thirdly, it would have altered the whole complexion of the Indian Mutiny, for without any great pressure on the resources of the engineers the shorter route could easily have been completed as far as Rajghât, on the banks of the river Ganges opposite Benares, before the summer of 1857. If this much had been accomplished, Benares, instead of Calcutta, would have formed our military base, the massacre of Cawnpore would have been unheard of and Lucknow would never have been besieged. Our troops would, in short, have only had to deal with Delhi, and the East Indian Railway would have been the means of saving at least half the bloodshed, and of terminating the struggle in quarter the time actually taken. When the Mutiny broke out the rail ended at Raneegunge, that is to say, within 121 miles of Calcutta, and when time meant everything and each day was precious, it took troops the best part of three weeks to march from the rail head to Benares, while the conveyance of stores and munitions of war took still longer.

At least two years were lost in discussion, but at last the decision was come to, to take the main line more or less along the course of the Ganges, the chief object being "to tap the river at Rajmahal." When, however, the railway got as far as Rajmahal, there was no river to tap, as in the meantime the Ganges had changed its course and the importance of Rajmahal had gone. But apart from this, the idea of making the main line *viâ* the loop and constructing a branch line to the Raneegunge coal field, committed the railway to an impossible course for its up-country coal traffic. It meant that all coal for Upper India had first to be conveyed fifty miles in a downward direction, and then had to be sent upwards by the roundabout loop line. To illustrate in some measure what this amounted to when put into mileage, it is only necessary to say that the opening of the present Chord line effected a saving of 146 miles between Raneegunge and Benares, while the opening of the Grand Chord line will mean the saving of another 50 miles between the same points.

On the other hand there is much to be said in favour of the decision to run the original main line along the fertile valley of the Ganges. Setting aside the fact that, before the days of railroads, the river was the chief means of transport and the main route of commerce, all the more important towns and trading centres such as Bhagulpur, Monghyr and Patna lay along its banks, and seeing that the first object of the railway, from a commercial point of view, was to secure traffic, it was most desirable that these towns should be served. They were the marts for the disposal of the produce of the adjoining districts, including the trans-Ganges districts which were then, of course, without railroads of any kind. It was more necessary to open out this part of the country than to run a railway through a coalfield, which, seeing that there was then but a small market for the disposal of coal, was unlikely to yield a traffic for many years; or to traverse an unprofitable route, at a time when the first need was to draw to the railway a traffic that existed and only needed to be secured and developed. Had the railway in the first instance been constructed through the hills of Hazaribagh, traversing a wild and thinly populated country, while the fertile and thickly peopled districts of the Gangetic plain were left untouched, there is little doubt that the financial success of the undertaking would have remained for a long period unassured. It is true that if, in the first instance, the main line of rail had followed the direct route, a branch line might have been constructed from, say, Gya to Patna, and that the East Indian Railway Company's Collieries at Giridih might have been reached in a reverse direction, from the vicinity of Parasnath, still the great districts bordering the best part of the Ganges would have been left untouched, and the whole of the traffic they contribute to the rail would have been lost.

On the whole therefore, the decision to run the original main line *viâ* the loop was a wise one, notwithstanding the fact that this route involved the crossing of all the waterways which drained into the Ganges, and so necessitated an enormous amount of bridging; notwithstanding also that it was the more expensive route to construct. It may also be said that had this route not been followed by the East Indian Railway at the outset, another company would certainly have stepped in; the Great Western of Bengal Railway was in fact formed with this very object.

An alternative which does not appear to have been discussed, but has occurred to the writer, would have been to continue the loop line as far as Moghalsarai and to construct the main line by the route which the Grand Chord will follow. This would have saved the construction of the present Chord between Sitarampur and Luckieserai, a section of the line which is not at all profitable, except for the Giridih branch, which could have been constructed in the reverse direction.

The loop line had not been opened long when the necessity for the Chord or present main line was established, and its construction decided upon; it would have been a fatal error if, instead of constructing the Chord line, the single line along the loop had, as some proposed, been doubled. It was enough that, at a time when railroads in India were mere experiments, the embankments and bridges of the loop were constructed to carry a double line, though to this day a single line is ample for its traffic requirements.

In the meantime other questions as to alignment arose, the more important being that in relation to the route to be followed between Agra and Delhi. It was at first decided to cross the Jumna at Agra and to run the line along the right bank of that river to Delhi; this was indeed the more direct route and work was actually started on it, part of the embankment being in evidence to this day. Before, however, any rails were laid, a discussion arose and as a consequence a change was introduced; the Government decided that the better course was to construct a branch line to Agra, in the same way that a branch line had been constructed to the river Ganges opposite Benares, and that the main line should be taken along the Ganges Doab, that is to say, between the Ganges and Jumna rivers, crossing the latter at Delhi instead of at Agra. Here again the great advantage was that more important towns would be served, and a still more fertile country traversed, than by following the shorter and more direct route along the right bank of the Jumna. These being the facts it seems particularly unjust that years afterwards, overlooking the claims of the East Indian, the construction of the direct line between Agra and Delhi should have been given by Government to a competing railway; yet this is what has been done and a Western India line now owns the route originally proposed by the East Indian Railway, and competes for its traffic.

Having reached Delhi the primary object of the East Indian Railway was accomplished. It is unnecessary to refer again to the controversy as to the entry into Delhi and the proposal that the East Indian Railway should be continued to Lahore, we know how these questions were settled; it is enough to say that, at the time, the Directors were satisfied with what had been accomplished, and that until after the appointment of General Sir Richard Strachey as Chairman of the Board, nothing more in the way of extension or construction was undertaken, although, as indicated elsewhere, the claim of the East Indian Railway to construct the Grand Chord line was, from time to time, strongly pressed on the Government. The story of the Grand Chord line is dealt with in another chapter; it would have been hard indeed had the making of this route been also entrusted to another system.

Time passed, and the construction of other railways proceeded apace. The Government of India came to the conclusion that in order to open up those parts of the country, off the main routes, where traffic was not likely to be heavy, certain railways should be constructed on the metre gauge, instead of on the broad gauge which had been accepted as the standard when railway construction began. In this way the Rajputana Railway came into existence and has ever since been saddled with the transhipment difficulty, at every point at which it joins a broad gauge line; a severe handicap in many ways, but particularly so where competition exists. There are few who doubt now that metre gauge lines should only be constructed as feeders to broad gauge railways, but so far as the writer knows, there is no definite policy in the matter.

In their anxiety to make railways cheaply, the Government also sanctioned a metre gauge railway between Muttra and Hathras, which was afterwards extended to Agra on the one side and to Cawnpore on the other. This line was made within the sphere of influence of the East Indian and at once started to compete for its traffic. How it was that the East Indian Railway failed to protest against the scheme is not clear, but it is evident that this line should have been constructed on the broad gauge, as part of the East Indian system which it crosses.

In 1889 a Company was formed to connect the East Indian Railway with the summer head-quarters of the Government of India in Simla. This line, starting from Delhi and terminating at Kalka at the foot of the Simla hills, is known as the Delhi-Umballa-Kalka Railway, and is worked by the East Indian as part of its system. Since then a Railway on a 2' 6" gauge has been constructed between Kalka and Simla which is managed as a separate concern, but has not so far proved a financial success; the cost of its construction seems to have been a great deal heavier than at first anticipated, while its traffic is inconsiderable.

The South Behar Railway which runs from Luckieserai Junction to Gya is another line constructed by a company but worked by the East Indian, and in the same way the East Indian works the Tarkessur Railway, a short branch from Sheoraphuli to Tarkessur. The Patna-Gya line originally constructed by the State and worked as a State line, and the branch from Nalhati to Azimgunge, which had also become a State Railway before it was handed over to the East Indian and its gauge altered, are now incorporated with the East Indian, and there is little doubt that the South Behar should be treated in the same way.

CHAPTER V.

TRADE DEPRESSION—MR. A. M. RENDEL VISITS INDIA AGAIN AND CRITICISES THE WORKING OF THE EAST INDIAN RAILWAY—ESTABLISHMENT OF A PROVIDENT FUND.

FOLLOWING several years of progress and successive seasons of increase, a temporary check set in in 1867. The period was marked by extreme depression in trade, and added to this the country was visited by abnormal floods, rendering the roads to the stations impassable for heavy traffic. The cotton boom of 1866, which had done so much to increase the receipts that year, was at an end, and under all heads of merchandise there was a falling off, though fortunately the passenger traffic continued to grow.

This change in the march of progress at once drew attention to the question of expenditure, and the point was raised whether it was really necessary or desirable to proceed with all the different works that had been sanctioned. Mr. A. M. Rendel, the Company's Consulting Engineer, was accordingly deputed to visit India again, to investigate the question on the spot, in communication with the officers of the Company and of the Government, and to consider in regard to works in contemplation or in course of execution, whether they should be proceeded with or deferred. Mr. Rendel proceeded to India in November 1867, and returning in March 1868, submitted a very full report on the various matters relating to his mission. He found that the great growth in expenditure during the preceding two years had been in advance of the natural development of the traffic, and as a consequence, many works which were projected, when it seemed that the power of the Railway to carry traffic was the sole limit to its use, were indefinitely postponed. Among others the doubling of the line between Gahmar station and Allahabad was deferred resulting in a saving of about £527,000. He reviewed the question relating to the construction of a bridge across the Hooghly river at Calcutta; dealt with the detail of duty performed by rolling-stock, stated his view that the mileage run was out of proportion to the work done and criticised the working generally. He advocated mixed trains and a reduction in the third class fare from 3 to $2\frac{1}{2}$ pie per mile, and investigated fuel consumption and numerous other matters. He also advocated that the whole line should be placed under one, instead of three chief Engineers, examined generally the establishment employed and proposed certain rules relating to the salaries of the staff and so forth. He altered the form of statistics shewing cost of working the line and made many suggestions which could not fail to be beneficial, and were for the most part adopted.

At this time one of the most difficult questions which had presented itself to the Board, in the organisation and management of the staff in India, had been how to meet the claims constantly urged for the payment of pensions, after a given period of service, founded upon the analogy of the Government services. The Company's European staff consisted of gentlemen, drawn chiefly from the best managed English lines, and it was felt that, without some retiring provision being made for them, the railway service in India did not form sufficient attraction. Various schemes, with a view to make the service more popular, were suggested, both at home and in India, but until 1867 every such proposition was found, from one cause or another, to be impracticable. In that year the conclusion was come to, after much anxious consideration, that the best mode of meeting the difficulty was to establish a Provident Fund, in the advantages of which all the servants of the Company, European and native, receiving a monthly pay of Rs. 30 and upwards should participate, the Fund being supported by contributions from the staff, assisted by the Company.

It was proposed:—

1st. That the present staff shall contribute to the Fund only if they think fit; but that all persons joining the service on and from a given date, with a monthly pay of Rs. 30 or over, and those who may be promoted to this pay, shall be required to do so.

2nd. That the staff shall be divided into two Classes—Class A consisting of all European servants of the Company and Class B comprising all servants of the Company not Europeans.

3rd. That those in Class A shall contribute 5 per cent. and those in Class B 2½ per cent. on their respective monthly salaries.

4th. That the Company shall contribute annually 1 per cent. on the surplus net earnings, after 6 per cent. per annum has been appropriated to the Company and the Government, in the terms of their contract, together with 1 per cent. on the 6 per cent. so appropriated so far as the surplus will admit of the said contributions.

5th. That the monies of the Fund shall be invested, from time to time, either in Indian Government securities or in railway stock, and that subject to rules and regulations to be prescribed by the Board, the Fund and all accruing interest shall be the property of the respective members of the staff in the ratio of their subscriptions.

Such were the rules of the original Provident Fund. Its creation was beneficial to the staff in numerous ways and it had the effect of giving every servant a direct personal interest in the economical working of the line, but it has never to this day given any employee a sufficient retiring allowance, and although various changes have been made in the original scheme, all of which have been introduced with the object of assisting the subscribers, a strong feeling exists that something more is needed.

In 1867 overtures were made to the Board to take over the Nalhati Branch Railway, constructed by a company known as the Indian Branch Railway Company, but the Board then declined to entertain them, as they were not prepared at the time "to construct or work any more branch lines." It was not until about 30 years afterwards that this railway, which in the meantime had been transferred to the State and was known as the Nalhati State Railway, was taken over by the East Indian and converted into a broad gauge line. It is known now as the Azimgunge branch line, and is part and parcel of the undertaking.

The Jubbulpore line was opened on the 1st August, 1867, before the Great Indian Peninsular Railway was ready to connect, and in the same year it was decided to construct a road bridge between Howrah and Calcutta, though whether this work should be undertaken by direct Government agency, or committed to the Municipality with Government assistance, was not then settled.

During the second half year of 1868 the traffic shewed signs of reviving and the net receipts of the year exceeded those of 1866, but the depression was not yet over and the development of traffic for some time was very gradual.

The following statement shews the net earnings of the Company from 1866 to 1869 inclusive :—

	£	s.	d.
1866	1,119,315	6	2
1867	1,076,741	12	8
1868	1,217,620	16	2
1869	1,446,322	6	10

The increases shewn in the net earnings would not have been so great but for the fact that working expenses were considerably reduced. By 1869 they had been brought down to 41·57 per cent. of the gross earnings. In this year the number of passengers carried was 4,911,018 and the weight of goods and minerals 1,261,113 tons.

In 1869 the East Indian Railway Volunteer Rifle Corps was formed, Mr. Edward Palmer, the Agent, was the first Honorary Colonel and about 416 servants of the Company at once enrolled themselves. The number of members has since increased very greatly and the corps is now over 2,300 strong with very few inefficients.

CHAPTER VI.

OPENING OF THE CHORD LINE FOLLOWED BY A TEMPORARY SLUMP IN TRAFFIC—THE BENGAL FAMINE OF 1873-4—REDUCTIONS IN RATES—COAL EXPORTED FROM CALCUTTA—ANALYSIS OF STATISTICS INTRODUCED.

THE year 1870 opened with the Chord line still awaiting completion, but otherwise this was the only important work of construction that remained unfinished.

The Chord line was opened for public traffic on the 1st January 1871, and on this date the work of constructing the East Indian Railway was considered to have ended. The engagements of all engineers not required for the maintenance of the line were now terminated, and the Board directed that the permanent staff should "be fixed at the lowest scale consistent with the nature of the duties to be performed."

The opening of the Chord route increased the mileage of the Railway to 1,280 miles—400 miles being double and 880 miles single—but no sooner had the Railway been thus far completed than a serious decline in traffic set in. The tonnage of goods and minerals carried during the first half of 1871 was 580,378 tons, against 700,804 tons in the corresponding half year of 1870. The

Company's goods sheds were empty, its wagons lay idle in sidings and many of its engines were put out of running. The Government of India were so concerned that they appointed a Committee to investigate the cause.

But there were no doubts as to the chief reasons of the decrease; in 1870 an exceptionally large famine traffic had been carried in consequence of a scarcity in the North-West Provinces, while the export seed trade of 1871 was much smaller than in the preceding year, because of a dull market in Calcutta, and because, in the words of the Board, the merchants, whenever the market was dull, "preferred the somewhat cheaper though more dilatory conveyance afforded by the river, which, owing to a very heavy rainfall, became navigable at an earlier period of the year than usual." Then again the Board tell us of another cause of decreased traffic, which is curious reading in these days, "the importations of English coal at Calcutta, as compared with any previous period since the Railway has been opened, have been so large as to have successfully competed in price with native coal, and have unquestionably very seriously interfered with the market for the latter."

The Committee appointed by Government do not appear to have thrown any fresh light on the question, but there is little doubt that the rates charged at the time were excessive, or traffic would not have fluctuated as it did between the river and the rail. A change in the mode of regulating the charge for carriage was sorely needed, though the point was not seriously taken up until some years later, when the experiences of a serious famine shewed what the possibilities were. Greater attention seems, however, to have been paid to lowering the cost of transport, and a further reduction in the working expenses followed. In the first half of 1872 these were brought down to 38·66 per cent. of the gross earnings and in 1873 to 37 per cent.

In 1873 Mr. E. Palmer, who had succeeded Sir Macdonald Stephenson in May 1857 and had held the office of sole Agent until 1866, when a fresh Board of Agency, of which he became Chairman, was constituted, retired. Mr. Palmer left the East Indian Railway, the foremost line in India for financial success, and in the words of the Consulting Engineer to the Government of India, "second to none in vigour of administration." The Government of India also expressed their appreciation of Mr. Palmer's "long and loyal service and high character."

The Agency was now reconstructed, and instead of consisting of three members, was conducted by two only, Messrs. Cecil Stephenson and George Sibley.

Owing to a failure of the rains in 1873 a famine occurred in Bengal, and the following extract from Mr. Crawford's address to the shareholders indicates the measures taken by the Government of India and the Railway Company to assist the people during that calamity :—

"The Directors had placed the line at the disposal of the Government. The Railway rate was ⅝d. per ton per mile, but the Government was sending the people provisions at a much less carriage charge than that, and made up the deficiency to the Company. Apart, however, from all questions of profit, it was a source of sincere gratification to the Directors, that they were able to render substantial assistance to the Government, in supplying the population of Bengal with food. Giving the Government the assistance of all their locomotive plant, they were enabled to deliver 4,000 tons of grain daily for the use of the people."

From the 1st November 1873 to the 3rd September 1874, the quantity of food grains carried into the famine-stricken districts and delivered at stations between Rajmahal and Arrah, was estimated at nearly seven hundred and fifty thousand tons. The traffic consisted chiefly of rice from Howrah, and of other grain from the North-West Provinces, and was consigned partly on Government and partly on private account.

In order to convey and accommodate so large an addition to the ordinary business of the Company, some thirty additional engines were erected and brought into use ; forty-six drivers and firemen were sent out from England, and ten were lent by the Madras Railway ; wagons were hired from the Bombay Baroda and Central India Railway ; the staff of guards was largely augmented ; watchmen were engaged to protect the grain lying at stations; and sidings to the river Ganges were laid, for the use of the Government, at Mokameh, Barh, and Futwah.

The half-yearly report of the Directors referring to this subject states that "the desire of the Board effectively to support the efforts of the Government in coping successfully with this, perhaps the greatest exigency of modern times, has been most ably and efficiently seconded and sustained throughout, by the unwearied and zealous co-operation of the whole of the service." Put in another way the East Indian Railway had been the main instrument by which a dire calamity had been prevented from attaining the proportions of a fearful catastrophe. This had been done without any interference whatever with the regular traffic of the country and at a rate which left no burden upon the Indian exchequer. The Railway, it was alleged, "was not a competitor with the river Ganges for the supply of the food required by the starving population, but merely another instrument in the hands of the Government for accomplishing their object."

As a result of the Bengal famine, considerable attention was given to the grain rates, and the wants of the different districts served by the Railway were carefully studied with a view to developing traffic generally. Perhaps the most important lesson learnt was that, in the upper part of India, there was a very large growth of grain and especially of wheat, a good deal of which found its way down the river Indus to the sea at Kurrachee. In a favourable season there was an immense surplus to dispose of and efforts were made to draw this produce to Calcutta, by quoting lower rates for its carriage than had previously been thought of. These efforts proved in a large measure successful; by introducing considerably reduced grain rates, a valuable traffic was drawn to the line and a profitable business established.

The only section of the Railway which was not doing so well as anticipated was the Jubbulpore branch, its local traffic was poor and the traffic interchanged with the Great Indian Peninsular Railway nominal. The Chairman said in his address in July 1874, "the Jubbulpore line must be considered for the present in the light of a political line, and it is very useful to travellers; but as regards the trade and commerce of the country, the line has not done much." The Jubbulpore branch runs for the most part through an uncultivated waste, poorly populated, and has always been the least paying portion of the Railway.

In 1873 some Bengal coal was taken by Madras for the use of the Madras Railway, and some was conveyed to Singapore for the manufacture of gas, and some to Bombay for cotton spinning works. The quantity exported was small, but this was the first recorded trade in export coal and at the time quite a new feature in the traffic. While on the subject of coal, it is well to say a few words as to the result of opening the Chord line route. It will be remembered that one of the reasons for constructing this route was that it would have the effect of bringing the Bengal coalfields nearer to the centre of the Company's system. The policy of the Board had often been questioned on the score of the initial expense, and on the grounds that the Chord route ran through an unprofitable tract of country, which its opponents thought was adequately served by the original branch line to the Raneegunge collieries. In 1875 Mr. Crawford in his address to the shareholders dwelt on this subject; he said :—

"They might now look upon the policy involved in the construction of that line with the utmost satisfaction. It had placed at their command that ample and abundant supply of fuel, which had enabled them to carry on their operations, without any fear whatever of being brought into difficulty for want of it."

Not only did the Chord line place at the service of the Company and of the public, including foreign railways, a vast quantity of easily accessible coal, but in opening out new sources of supply, it brought about, not only reduction in cost, but a better quality of fuel than that obtainable from Raneegunge itself.

During 1875 considerable changes were made in the personnel of the administration Calcutta, Mr. Cecil Stephenson, Chief

Agent, died, and Mr. Sibley, who had been Chief Engineer for many years, retired, and seeing that all construction works of any magnitude were at an end, it was thought unnecessary to retain the services of both an Agent and a Chief Engineer. Mr. Bradford Leslie, now Sir Bradford Leslie, who had formerly been Chief Engineer of the Eastern Bengal Railway Company and had afterwards been employed in building the floating road bridge over the Hooghly, was selected to fill the dual appointment of Agent and Chief Engineer.

Shortly after Mr. Cecil Stephenson's death a tablet to his memory was placed on the wall of Howrah Station and a copy of the inscription on it is here given :—

IN MEMORY OF
CECIL MACKINTOSH STEPHENSON.
AGENT OF THE
EAST INDIAN RAILWAY COMPANY,
WHO DIED AT SEA ON THE 21ST NOVEMBER 1875, AGED 56.
THIS TABLET IS ERECTED
AS A MARK OF THEIR SINCERE ESTEEM AND RESPECT
BY MORE THAN FIVE THOUSAND OFFICERS AND MEN
OF THE EAST INDIAN RAILWAY
(AND OTHERS DESIRING TO JOIN),
WHO HAVE ALSO PLACED A SIMILAR TABLET
IN THE CALCUTTA CATHEDRAL,
AND INSTITUTED A SCHOLARSHIP
IN THE DIOCESAN SCHOOL AT NAINI TAL
FOR SONS OF EAST INDIAN RAILWAY
SERVANTS.

The following statement shows the net earnings of the Company from 1870 to 1875 inclusive:—

		£.	s.	d.
1870	…	1,549,628	17	0
1871	…	1,380,377	1	5
1872	…	1,483,385	0	11
1873	…	1,686,338	6	2
1874	…	2,196,877	1	5
1875	…	1,624,333	6	3

The figures combine the earnings of the main and Jubbulpore lines, though at this time the accounts were separately kept, and are interesting as shewing the effect of the famine traffic of 1873-74. They also shew, excluding the two exceptionally poor years, 1871-72, when trade was more or less stagnant and everything depressed, that following the famine there was a distinct development.

In 1871 we find for the first time an analysis of statistical figures much in the form in which they are given at the present time. The principle of these statistics was laid down by Sir Alexander Rendel (then Mr. Rendel) in conjunction with Colonel Strachey, R.E., now Sir Richard Strachey, Chairman of the Board, and will be referred to in greater detail elsewhere. It is sufficient to say here that according to the first analysis the average load of a goods train on the main line was 109 tons and on the Jubbulpore branch 68 tons. At the present time an average load of under 275 tons is considered poor.

CHAPTER VII.

VISIT OF THE PRINCE OF WALES TO INDIA—REDUCTIONS IN RATES—ECONOMIES IN WORKING.—THE MADRAS FAMINE AND SHORTAGE OF STOCK—GENERAL STRACHEY VISITS INDIA.—THE GIRIDIH COLLIERIES—PROSPERITY OF THE UNDERTAKING.

IN 1875-1876 His Royal Highness the Prince of Wales visited India and great preparations were made to afford him a Royal welcome. That the efforts made to ensure his comfort while travelling on the East Indian Railway were successful, is proved by the following extract from the *Gazette of India*, dated 22nd April 1876 :—

"On the East Indian Railway, His Royal Highness the Prince of Wales travelled in January 1876 from Howrah to Bankipore, and thence to Benares, also from Cawnpore to Delhi ; and from Delhi to Ghaziabad, on going to the Punjab, and from Ghaziabad to Agra in returning thence. In February, His Royal Highness travelled from Agra to Aligarh, and in March from Cawnpore to Allahabad and on to Jubbulpore.

The orders issued concerning the details of working the Royal train by the authorities of the East Indian Railway were such as to ensure punctuality in running, combined with all possible precautions for safety.

On the conclusion of the journey to Jubbulpore, His Royal Highness was pleased to acknowledge his thanks personally to the Officiating Agent and Traffic Manager for their attention to him, and to commend the railway arrangements in connection with the several State ceremonials of arrival and departure of trains during the different journeys made upon the line by His Royal Highness."

The visit of His Royal Highness the Prince of Wales resulted in a concourse of Native Princes and others visiting Calcutta, and led to a considerable increase in receipts from passenger traffic, but as a set-off there was a certain outgoing to be taken into account under the head of carriage building and outward demonstrations; a special train had to be constructed, as the Prince of Wales could not be sent about in an ordinary carriage, and stations had to be decorated in token of loyalty; all this cost money, but the Chairman in analysing the financial result to the Railway said : " I dare say we may put it down that if His Royal Highness had not gone to India we should have been about £40,000 worse off than we are." Seeing that the special train constructed for the Prince of Wales, was used for the next twenty-five years as the Viceregal train, this result was by no means unsatisfactory.

About the same time Mr. A. M. Rendel again visited India. The completion by the Government of the bridge over the Hooghly, between Howrah and Calcutta having rendered necessary considerable alterations at the Howrah terminus, Mr. Rendel was deputed to investigate the requirements of the case on the spot Mr. Rendel not only dealt with the question of Howrah station but went over the whole line from one end to the other and settled various details with the Company's officers in India.

Reference has been made in a previous chapter to the effect of the Bengal famine on the question of goods rates. Mr. Crawford, the Chairman of the Board of Directors, referred to this in his address to the shareholders in January 1877 ; he said—

"The experience of the famine traffic had shewn us that there was an enormous production of the soil in India of a very valuable character, but which had been for the most part necessarily retained in the districts in which it was grown, for the want of any other market than the local markets of the neighbourhood."

This was in some measure true, but we have seen already that a good deal of the surplus production of the soil found its way to the seaboard by river, and particularly by the river Indus to Kurrachee. In 1876 the Government took off the export dues, which up till then had militated against a really large export trade, and at about the same time silver began to decline in value. The depreciation of silver assisted the export of country produce and some encouragement in railway rates was alone needed to draw the traffic to the Railway. Reductions were accordingly made, and as Mr. Crawford in another part of his address added :—

"The effect of the reduction of the rates was to enable purchasers of wheat at Cawnpore, 684 miles from Calcutta, to rely upon their being able to get their wheat down to Calcutta for a sum not exceeding about 6s. 4d. per quarter. That taken into account with other elements of reduced cost has led to a very great and important increase in the trade of grain between India and this country. The same has been the case with seeds. The duty of the company was to assist by reduction of charge in facilitating the removal of this large produce of grain and seeds and our rates have enabled merchants to bring their wheat to England, together with their linseed and other seeds, at a cost which could not have been possible a very short time before."

"I do not see anything in the conditions in which this traffic has been carried on to deter me from expecting a continuance of it."

At about the same time arrangements were concluded with the line then known as "the Sindh, Punjab and Delhi Railway," by which purchasers of grain in the Punjab were able to bring their grain to Calcutta, a distance of 1,245 miles, at a cost of about 12s. 9d. per quarter, a rate which was then considered remarkably low. As illustrating the growth of the export wheat trade, the following figures of exports from Calcutta are interesting, more than one-half being brought down by the East Indian Railway :—

Years.	Tons exported.
1874	18,926
1875	58,532
1876	170,240

The company was now enjoying a period of activity, and prospects were undoubtedly encouraging. The Railway was about 25 years old and past experience justified the feeling that it would continue to prove one of the grandest undertakings in the world's history. But the success of the East Indian Railway was not entirely owing to the measures taken to develop traffic; a large share of its prosperity was due to the economical conditions under which the line was worked. Mr. Crawford at the same meeting said, "we should never have arrived at a satisfactory net result, if our efforts on this side to inculcate economy had not been most actively and honestly supported on the other side." His remarks had special reference to an outcry raised by the Indian newspapers of the day, as to the alleged injustice of replacing European by native labour. Mr. David Campbell, the Locomotive Superintendent, had recently promoted about 87 native firemen to appointments, previously held by Europeans, as shunters and drivers of goods trains on branch lines, with most satisfactory results. The experiment carried out in the face of much opposition led to a considerable economy and naturally had the full support of the Board.

Another economy introduced in 1877 was in connection with the maintenance of the telegraph. The Railway had established a line of telegraph wire on one side of the line, and the Government had a line of telegraph on the other side. This necessitated two telegraphic establishments, and it was obviously a waste of money that one establishment should be employed in keeping in order and repair the line on one side, while another establishment should be engaged in looking after the wires on the other. An arrangement was therefore come to with the Government, under which they undertook the repair and maintenance of the railway wires, and the Railway had no longer to keep up a staff of its own for the purpose.

A failure of the rains of 1876 led to another famine in India, this time in the Madras and Bombay Presidencies. A strong demand for food grains, pulses and rice set in in October 1876, and continued unabated almost throughout 1877. The great bulk of the traffic flowed over the East Indian Railway from the North-West Provinces and the Punjab, the largest proportion going *viâ* the Jubbulpore line and the Great Indian Peninsula Railway, but there was also a heavy traffic to Howrah, for transmission to Madras by sea.

At the same time there was a large wheat and seed export trade, and consequently the usual sequence of a shortage of wagon supply. The papers in India teemed with expressions of disapproval of the East Indian Railway management, because it had not sufficient stock to meet the extraordinary demands made upon it. The facts were that the stock of wagons had amply sufficed to meet the famine requirements of 1873-74, but when it came to sending East Indian Railway wagons hundreds of miles away from the home line to distant Madras, it became impossible to meet all demands. Out of a total stock of 6,600 goods wagons, as many as 1,200 or say one-fifth were constantly absent from the line, conveying produce to the Bombay or Madras Presidencies. There would have been an abundant supply of wagons to carry our own traffic but there were not sufficient to carry grain to Madras as well as to Calcutta, and obviously it was beyond the bounds of possibility to meet this exceptional demand. The Board however at once applied for Government sanction to the provision of 1,000 more wagons and 50 additional engines, at a cost of a quarter of a million of money, and sanction was accorded after some short delay.

Towards the close of 1877 and at the beginning of 1878 shareholders were beginning to enquire what action the Government intended to take in respect to the purchase of the Railway. Mr. Crawford, although he could then make no official announcement, had already taken up the question and was in communication with the Government as to its intentions. The position was that on the 15th February 1879, and for six months afterwards, the Government had the power of giving notice to the Company of its intention to purchase the property, such intention to take effect on the expiration of six months' notice. The terms of purchase were the average market value of the stock of the Company for three years preceding the date on which such notice should be given. There was much conjecture as to the course the Government would follow, and when it was announced, early in 1878, that Lieut.-Genl. Strachey, R. E., a member of the Council of the Secretary of State for India, had proceeded to

Calcutta to consider, "with the Government and Railway authorities on the spot, certain propositions for the completion of the Company's system," it was not unnatural to associate his visit with the question of Government purchase of the Railway.

The Board thought it desirable that Mr. A. M. Rendel, the Consulting Engineer to the Company, should also proceed to India and take part in the enquiries to be made by General Strachey, as, setting aside the question of purchase, there were many important matters requiring decision. The rapidity with which traffic had developed in recent years rendered it essential to decide, without delay, what further facilities should be provided. In other words it had become very necessary that accurate information should be obtained as to the works needed to enable the Railway to meet the development of traffic. Among these works were the carrying of the line over the river Hooghly by a bridge at a convenient point above Calcutta, the idea then being to construct a passenger station in the Metropolis and so leave the whole of the Howrah property for the wheat, seeds and coal trade. Then again, there were the questions of extending the double line and of bridging the Ganges at or near Benares, so as to make a better connection with the Oudh and Rohilkhand Railway. These were big questions and there were many others of minor importance.

It is not necessary here to refer in any detail to this visit of Genl. Strachey and Mr. Rendel to India. Genl. Strachey's visit was undoubtedly in connection with the question of Government taking over the East Indian Railway, and this will be more fully dealt with in another chapter. Mr. Rendel as usual submitted a very full report as soon as he returned, dealing with the engineering questions above referred to, but no proposals were made by the Board to the Government to enter upon the works recommended by him, because the intentions of Government in regard to the purchase of the line were not known until some time afterwards. Suffice to say here that in 1879 a Bill was presented in Parliament "to enable the Secretary of State in Council to enter into contracts for the purchase of the undertaking of the East Indian Railway Company and for other purposes in relation to such Company." This Bill received the Royal assent on the 11th August 1879, and under its provisions a contract, to continue in force for a period of not less than 20 years from the 1st January 1880, was entered into, embodying the conditions on which the undertaking was continued in the hands of the Company.

Before giving any details of the growth of traffic during the period immediately preceding the purchase of the Railway by the State, there are one or two incidents to record. In 1878 the Company lost, through death, the services of two of its most valued officers. Mr. Robert Roberts, the Chief Auditor, died at Alexandria on his way to England, after a service of eighteen years, and was succeeded by Mr. R. C. S. Mackenzie, the first assistant of the Department. Mr. J. C. Batchelor, who for nearly twenty years had discharged with ability and zeal the duties of Traffic Manager, died suddenly in Calcutta, and Mr. N. St. L. Carter, Deputy Traffic Manager, was appointed to fill the vacant post. It may here be mentioned that Mr. Batchelor was formerly an officer on the staff of the London and North Western Railway and was considered one of the most able Traffic Managers the East Indian Railway ever had.

The net earnings of the East Indian Railway Company from 1876 to 1879 inclusive were:—

1876 ...	...	£2,110,286 10 4
1877 ...	...	2,770,667 11 10
1878 ...	...	2,344,942 9 0
1879 ...	...	2,665,751 16 7

Prior to the year 1876 wheat exports from India had been comparatively small, but in that year there was so great an advance in the trade that British India, instead of being at the bottom, took the third place in the list of countries from which the United Kingdom drew its supply, and there was every indication of a still further increase in despatches as facilities were enlarged and made available to commerce. The seed traffic was also growing in importance, but more important than either of these two was the, as yet, almost undeveloped coal traffic. It is true that it had already reached some magnitude, and was gradually growing, but this was chiefly due to the requirements of railways, which had to take coal, and not to the creation of an export trade, which followed years afterwards when a more suitable tariff was introduced. In 1876 there was very little demand for local coal for seagoing steamers, and the chief consideration of the time seems to have been moderately cheap fuel for railway consumption.

The quantity of coal carried for the public during the three years ending 1876 was

1874	Tons	505,519
1875	,,	515,846
1876	,,	520,262

Now in connection with the coal traffic of these days it must be remembered that the East Indian Railway collieries supplied a large portion of the public demand. The Giridih coalfield was discovered in the early years of the history of the East Indian Railway, and, thanks to the intelligence and foresight of Mr. (afterwards Sir) Macdonald Stephenson, the East Indian Railway Company acquired control over it. At one time there was a sharp controversy between the Government and the Company as to the use of this coal-field. The Government said they could not allow guaranteed capital to be used in working a coal mine, and in fact gave orders that the mines were to be closed. What followed is best described in Mr. Crawford's words:—"We on our part were not prepared to submit to this, and as the Government would not alter their determination we brought out what was called 'The Auxiliary Railway Company,' by which we proposed to make the Chord line, and to develop the Giridih property. A letter was written to Sir Charles Wood, in which we pointed out to him, from what I may call the commercial aspect of the case, how absolutely necessary it was that we should take the course we proposed to take. We told him the great advantages that in our judgment would arise from it. Sir Charles Wood gave way, authority was given to make the Chord line, to get access to these mines, and you see the result. We get our coal at 7s. 5d. a ton."

It was not, however, the East Indian Railway that alone benefited by the cheap coal made available by the construction of the Chord line. The East Indian Railway did not require for themselves all the coal that was raised from their mines, and was able to place at the disposal of Government and of other railways connecting with them, the whole of their surplus raisings, for which cost price was charged in addition to railway freight. There were, however, other coal-owners in India besides the Railway

Company, and these people took exception to the course pursued by the Company and, in the words of Mr. Crawford, threatened "all manner of things." "They talk," he said, "of getting an interdict from the Government. In fact they threaten legal proceedings; but they are not aware of this, that we are entitled under our constitution to work and to win and to make profit out of coal and minerals. It was one of those things for which we are indebted to the foresight of our colleague, Sir Macdonald Stephenson, who after thirty years' connection with us, is still happily with us. He foresaw the advantages that would arise from this; therefore in the deed of contract we have the power to do these things, and that deed has been approved by Government; there is therefore no doubt as to our legal authority to deal if we choose in coal. How we came to possess the coal was in this way. We were engaged some twenty-five years ago in constructing our line along the Ganges, where a large quantity of brickwork was to be done. Our people were at their wits' end for fuel wherewith to burn the bricks. As the Americans say, they prospected the country, and it resulted in finding coal. When found, Sir Macdonald Stephenson took measures immediately to acquire control over the coal. That was obtained and we have now legal control over the coal pits. There are other coal deposits, and other people can work them if they like, as well as ourselves. Our purpose in relation to coal is this—to use as much as we require for our own purposes at the smallest cost, having done this we wish to supply our neighbours with as much coal as we can, they paying us merely the profits of carriage. There is the Oudh and Rohilkhand, which is comparatively speaking our nearest neighbour in one direction, and I hope we shall be able to keep them continually supplied with the coal they require on terms satisfactory to them, and the same with the Great Indian Peninsular."

How the controversy regarding the sale by the Railway of its surplus coal ended it is needless to recapitulate, at the time the words were spoken the Company was on the eve of negotiations with Government as to its future. It was feared that the Government might not only purchase the undertaking but work it also. Mr. Crawford held the view, apparently accepted by Government, that "no railway of this magnitude is likely to succeed if it is administered by departmental officers of Government." The Railway was already paying the Government handsome profits, in the year 1877 the Government share amounted to about £600,000, and on this Mr. Crawford said, "Gentlemen, if you will turn to the pages of a certain book called the Fables of Æsop, you will see the story of a countryman who was fortunate in possessing a goose which laid every day a golden egg ? You know what the countryman did with the goose. We, the East Indian Railway Co., are the goose ; the golden egg is the £600,000 which the Secretary of State will get out of this Railway for the year 1877 ; but whether Lord Salisbury will be the countryman or not remains for the future to discover."

Let us look for a moment at the goose as described by Mr. Crawford in a previous speech. It shews how the Railway was then regarded and what expectations were held for its future. He said " with regard to the undertaking itself, you will bear in mind that there is perhaps no railway enterprise upon the face of this earth, traversing so great a distance, that is more favourably placed than ours is. We have little or nothing to contend with in the way of unfavourable gradients ; we have a plain and level country to pass through. We have a river, it is true to compete with, but which I think will be found in the long run will be less of a competitor than a coadjutor with us. We serve a country densely peopled—a people living in a state of tranquility, who are able to devote themselves to the exercise of all the arts of life, whatever they may be, which they pursue, whether agriculture or manufactures or whatever else ; and we have arrived at that time now when the cultivators of the soil in India, and the traders into whose hands the produce of the cultivators passes, have found that the supply of every article, wherever produced along the East Indian line, exceeding the local consumption, is carried to market by rail. A man can enter upon the cultivation of land with confidence that his produce, if in excess of that required for the supply of the immediate neighbourhood, will find a market elsewhere. All this arises in a great measure from the fact that the produce there raised is of a kind readily taken by other people than the people of India. There are acres upon acres, districts of land in India, which are now covered with wheat cultivation. There are large areas in the lower, independently of the Upper Provinces of India, where the cultivation of oil seeds, linseed and rape seeds, and other things of that kind is carried on to a vast extent. There is nothing whatever in the ordinary circumstances of India which can prevent our enjoying to the full extent the full benefit as railway carriers."

During the period we are now dealing with the growth of the passenger traffic and the measures advisable to encourage it were also being considered. The increase in the passenger traffic was thought not so great as it might have been and the question of reducing the third class fare was a subject to which consideration was being given. Mr.

Crawford in his address to the shareholders in 1878 said :—

> "I do not know whether our rates are higher than they ought to be, but to carry a passenger eight miles for 3d. cannot inflict a very great burden upon him. The Southern of India Railway, I am told, however, carry passengers at two-thirds of our rates and their traffic is increasing. If that be the case it certainly behoves us to see how far the principle of lower fares can be applied with success upon our system. It is not to be forgotten that it is a dangerous question to meddle with, and we had better be cautious in what we do."

What was done a few years later is related elsewhere, in the meantime we need only mention that the Railway was carrying over six million passengers annually in 1875 and that, in 1879, the figures had gone up to more than seven and one half millions, of whom nearly seven millions were of the third class.

The working expenses were still decreasing, in the second half of 1879 the percentage to gross receipts for the main line was down to 31·86 and in whatever way regarded the general outlook was most favourable.

CHAPTER VIII.

OPENING OF THE RAJPUTANA RAILWAY LEADS TO COMPETITION BETWEEN CALCUTTA AND BOMBAY—THE VIEWS OF GOVERNMENT ON THE QUESTION—THE POSITION DEFINED BY MR. CRAWFORD, CHAIRMAN OF THE EAST INDIAN RAILWAY.

THE Rajputana-Malwa (metre gauge) Government Railway, connecting the North West Provinces with Bombay, viâ the Bombay, Baroda and Central India Railway, was opened for traffic on the 1st January 1881, and very shortly afterwards, the question of the competition between the Ports of Calcutta and Bombay came under the consideration of the Government of India, with a view to the laying down of principles upon which the traffic by the rival routes should be conducted, having due regard to the several interests concerned.

Taking the two important centres Agra and Delhi, distances to Bombay and Calcutta then compared :—

	Miles.
Agra to Bombay viâ Rajputana	847
,, ,, ,, viâ Jubbulpore	1,131
Agra to Calcutta	841
Delhi to Bombay viâ Rajputana	889
,, ,, ,, viâ Jubbulpore	1,234
Delhi to Calcutta	954

The Board of the East Indian Railway held that the Calcutta trade should be given the full advantage of the economical conditions under which their line was worked; they argued in fact that the East Indian Railway should have the power of carrying goods at cheaper rates than other railways.

The managements of the Bombay Baroda and Rajputana State Railways declined to accept this view, and undeterred by the disadvantage of break of gauge, at once began active competition by reducing charges, in order to draw to Bombay by their route, a large portion of the traffic which had previously been carried by the East Indian Railway, from Agra and Delhi, to Calcutta.

The Great Indian Peninsular Railway, which had previously only secured a small portion of the traffic of the North-West and Punjab to Bombay by the Jubbulpore route, found themselves seriously handicapped and proposed to construct an extension of their line to Cawnpore, which would shorten the distance by their route, both from Cawnpore and above. This proposal was accepted by the Secretary of State and thus a further complication was introduced, though it is true that it was not until some years later that the connection was actually made by the Indian Midland Railway, since amalgamated with the Great Indian Peninsular.

The Government of India wrote a despatch on the question in which the general principle was laid down that railway rates should be fixed "at the lowest limit possible to secure a fair profit on working." This principle was very much in accord with the views of the East Indian Railway Board, who now looked upon the competition with less alarm, for they knew they could make a fair profit out of far lower rates than other railways and therefore had the whip hand.

Let us, however, extract more fully from the Government despatch, which is dated 19th May 1882.

"The Government of India has certainly no wish to favour either the port of Calcutta or that of Bombay in this matter. Both ports have their respective advantages and disadvantages as regards the export of country produce. Bombay has a magnificent harbour and a convenient dock, combined with lower freight charges to Europe; but as regards inland transport it has the disadvantage of costly fuel and hilly country. Calcutta on the other hand has a somewhat dangerous river for its approach, no docks and heavier freight charges to Europe; but in respect of inland transport it has great advantages, not only from the abundant supply of cheap coal but also from its river transport. The competition of the river compels low charges on the railways, while the cheap coal enables these low charges to be remunerative; and it appears to His Excellency the Governor-General in Council that if the Government ruled that the rates from Delhi and Agra to Bombay and Calcutta were to be the same, such ruling would be distinctly favouring Bombay at the expense of Calcutta, and placing an artificial restriction on the East Indian Railway traffic, thereby depriving the districts served by it of the natural advantages of their position."

At this time the rates from Agra and Delhi to Calcutta and Bombay were considerably in favour of Calcutta, and the Government of India in this despatch merely reiterated the theory they had promulgated in a previous letter to the Government of Bombay, to the effect that "the ultimate limit of legitimate competition between the various lines must be regulated by their capabilities of making *an equally fair profit* from the traffic they carry."

A long controversy ensued in which the Chambers of Commerce in Calcutta and Bombay joined, while the Secretary of State expressed an opinion quite opposed to that held by the Government of India. He was in favour of leaving the rival railway lines to compete for the trade by quoting whatever rates they found desirable, subject to the interposition of Government in extreme cases, and laid down that "the advantages due either to geographical position or other circumstances, should furnish no reason for imposing on either artificial restrictions, in order to produce an equal return of net profits on the capital of both."

These very opposite views in no way brought the controversy to a close. It continued for years before even a temporary solution was come to, but ultimately the Government of India, in 1887, accepted in a large measure the principles laid down by the Secretary of State that "the managers of railways should be left to fix their own rates and fares, that the interests of railways and trade generally would be better served by accepting the legitimate consequences of competition, and that the interposition of Government would be justified only in cases where companies, under the security of a guarantee, might fix rates below what would cover the cost of transport with a margin of profit."

Certain general rules were then formulated by Government, subject to which railways were left free to fix such rates and fares as seemed most advantageous for their respective lines.

Among these rules were what is known as maximum and minimum rates, but otherwise the utmost latitude was allowed the several railway managements. In other words it was left to the railways to compete with each other, until they reached the minimum charge permissible, whether this minimum meant a profitable charge or otherwise. The natural result has been that in the course of years of competition, coupled with other considerations, the lines leading to Calcutta and Bombay have both reached the minimum in many instances, and the East Indian Railway, not being able to go further, loses the advantage that a purely commercial concern would gain by reason of the cheaper conditions under which it is worked.

As will be shewn further on the question has recently been revived, and is under discussion at the present moment; but while this correspondence was going on and at a time when the Rajputana route had started active competition with the East Indian Railway for the trade of the North West, and when the Great Indian Peninsular Railway was still endeavouring to gain access to Cawnpore, Mr. Crawford issued an interesting brochure entitled " Some Observations on the Development of the Railway System of the Valley of the Ganges."

In this sketch Mr. Crawford considered the general effect of the accomplishment of certain projects likely to affect the working of the East Indian Railway.

He referred firstly to the approaching completion of the Hooghly bridge, connecting the railways on either side of Calcutta; then to the bridge crossing the Ganges river at Benares and the probable acquirement by the Government of the Oudh and Rohilkand Railway; then to the development of the Bengal and North-Western Railway System, serving, with the Tirhoot State line, the important provinces north of the Ganges, and lastly to the competition between Bombay, Kurrachee and Calcutta.

It is only with the last portion of the pamphlet that we are here interested, and more particularly with the competition between Bombay and Calcutta.

" This competition," he remarked, " was unknown, in point of fact it was not possible, before the meeting of the East Indian and Great Indian Peninsular lines of Railway at Jubbulpore in the year 1869, and it has been effective only since the completion of the Rajputana-Malwa (narrow gauge lines) and their incorporation with the Bombay-Baroda line in 1881, thus affording Bombay a continuous unbroken communication with points of contact with the East Indian line at Agra and at Delhi. The basis upon which this competition is, as regards Bombay, the great superiority the port possesses over the port of Calcutta, owing mainly to natural causes—the extent and depth of the water of its harbour, its facility of access and immunity from cyclones and, more than all, its position, confronting, on the Western coast of India, the entrance to the Red Sea, and the communications with every part of Europe. Add to these the moderate port charges and there appears to be some reason why there should be a reputed difference of 10s. per ton in favour of Bombay, between the freights from Bombay and those from Calcutta, and just as much, say 10s. per ton in the relative costs of the transport of goods between the marts in upper India and their destination in Europe."

"If by the gifts of nature Bombay is so largely superior to Calcutta as a shipping port, there is a set off of no slight importance in the fact that the approach to, and departure from Bombay, are subject to the drawback of the Western Ghâts in both the lines of the Great Indian Peninsular Railway leading into the interior of the country, and the flooding of the rivers, notably the Taptee and Nurbudda, which cross the path of the Bombay and Baroda Railway, in its northward course to its junction with the Rajputana-Malwa line at Sabarmati. Added to this, coal is not to be found economically suitable for the purposes of locomotion at any point on either of these lines. The consequence is that both of these depend upon the imported coal into Bombay for the supply of their requirements, at a cost as follows compared with the East Indian Railway Company: thus the

		Half year ended 30th June 1885.
East Indian Railway used	... Tons	100,175
Great Indian Peninsular ,,	... ,,	108,490
Bombay and Baroda ,,	. ,,	24,987

Costing

East Indian Railway	Rs.	479,422
per ton at 1/8 per rupee	...	7s. 11¾d.
Great Indian Peninsular ...	Rs.	1,678,778
per ton at 1/8 per rupee	...	£1 5s. 9½d.
Bombay and Baroda	Rs	493,112
per ton at 1/8 per rupee	...	£1 12s. 10½d.

This statement showed that, in the one item of coal, the East Indian possessed an enormous and indisputable advantage over the Bombay lines, but if it was a fact that Bombay possessed a superiority in homeward freights it still remained necessary for the East Indian, by the observance of every practical economy in management, and by affording every possible facility to the public, to take all the advantage it could of its cheap working, and so retain the traffic to which it considered itself entitled.

The bridging of the Hooghly, the enlargement of Howrah station and the additions to locomotive and wagon stock then contemplated were among the measures which, in Mr. Crawford's words, enabled the East Indian Railway "to enter into a free and open competition with the Great Indian Peninsular and Bombay and Baroda Railways, confident of being able to hold their own, if they are only allowed fair play."

Taking the Great Indian Peninsular Railway first, their avowed object in getting into Cawnpore was to divert from the East Indian Railway as much as they could of the Cawnpore-Calcutta traffic.

"Cawnpore," wrote Mr. Crawford, "is distant from Calcutta 684 miles, and it will be, it is understood, 831 miles distant from Bombay, consequently the distance from Bombay to Calcutta by the two routes conjointly being 1515 miles, the half-way house or mid-point of the entire route will be at 757 miles from either port or about 31 miles distant westward of Calpee. In other words, all things being equal, a ton of goods could be sent from that half-way house to either port for the same charge for freight.

"But all things are not equal in this case of competition. If, on the one hand, the Western Port of India is unsupplied by nature with coal of any kind for the locomotive uses of the railways, and the courses of those Railways are impeded and obstructed by mountain ranges and the opposing waters of great rivers, we find, on the other hand, Calcutta in immediate connection with coal-fields of great extent on the very line of her chief Railway, and that railway pursuing its way of nearly 1000 miles to Delhi over a course practically level throughout.

"The results of these differences in the natural conditions under which the East Indian and the lines of Western

India are worked have been formulated in the Summary of the Analysis of Working of Indian Railways, and show—

Average cost of hauling a goods unit (one ton) one mile

East Indian Railway	pies 2·40
Great Indian Peninsular	„ 5·27
Bombay and Baroda	„ 4·77
Rajputana Railway	„ 5·20 "

This great difference in favour of the East Indian Railway was, in Mr. Crawford's opinion, " sufficient to transfer the central economical working meeting point on the Indian Midland line, 356 miles to the westward of Cawnpore."

In the competition with the united Bombay, Baroda and Rajputana Railways the case was somewhat different; the distance from Calcutta to Agra being 841 miles and from Bombay to Agra 847 miles, the midway house is 3½ miles to the west of Agra, or say at Agra itself, but according to Mr. Crawford's calculations the economical working midway point would be 307 miles westward of Agra.

These arguments, which are perfectly sound, apply with equal force to the present time. Beyond laying down maximum and minimum rates, the Government has, as already indicated, in no way interfered with competition between the different railways in India, the minimum rates are the same for all and, as a consequence, the Bombay lines charge from Agra to Bombay the same as the East Indian charges from Agra to Calcutta;

while from Cawnpore the Great Indian Peninsular and the East Indian have been known, during active competition, to both charge the minimum allowed them for the more important items of traffic, or in other words to maintain equal mileage rates irrespective of the cost of working. Therefore up to the present time the East Indian Railway has not been allowed to get any advantage from the more economical conditions under which it is worked. Such an arrangement is not only contrary to the spirit of commercial enterprise, but is distinctly unfair to the East Indian Railway. It is very doubtful whether the minimum rates can pay in the case of railways which are not so cheaply worked, and it would be interesting to hear what arguments there are to the contrary. It may also be remarked here that to protect the public by prescribing maximum rates, above which no railway may charge, is understandable, but that rates should be governed by minima, below which no railway may go, is an economic absurdity. Minimum rates were no doubt brought about by the system of Government guarantees, and the fear that, without some such restriction, certain railways would charge lower rates than were profitable to them, but this is no defence when it limits the powers of a railway, in a position to charge less than the prescribed minimum, and yet derive a fair margin of profit.

This question of competition will be referred to in other phases elsewhere; it is sufficient to say here that Mr. W. A. Dring, the present General Traffic Manager of the East Indian Railway, has in a recent note on slow freight rates re-opened the question of a varying minima and it is on this that we are now awaiting the decision of Government. Mr. Dring says :—

"The present minimum charge of ·23d per ton mile is acting as a restraint on the operations of the managements to which Government has entrusted the working of its railways, and it seems probable that in the early future Government may consider whether the minimum can be reduced. There will then be the problem whether, as hitherto, there shall be one minimum for all alike, or whether the cheap working lines shall be allowed to charge a lower rate than the system where the prevailing conditions do not permit of the same economy. In other words, whether the cost of working shall be taken into consideration in fixing the minimum rate which may be quoted by the different systems. It is too much to expect that there shall be a different minimum for each railway, small and large, but it is submitted that different minimum rates based on cost of working could be laid down for the larger systems, and a general minimum for the smaller, and that such a procedure would be both fair to the consignor whose goods are to be carried, and in the interests of Government as owning the railways."

CHAPTER IX.

NEGOTIATIONS PRECEDING THE PURCHASE OF THE EAST INDIAN RAILWAY BY GOVERNMENT.

THE negotiations which preceded, and gradually led up to the purchase of the East Indian Railway Company by Government, have been placed on record by Mr. Crawford, in a pamphlet published in 1880, entitled "A Short Account of the Preliminary Negotiations."

Towards the close of 1876, the first of the three years constituting the period of which the average price of the Company's stock in the market was to be taken as the value of the Railway, in the event of the Secretary of State electing to purchase the line, had nearly run its course, and the time had arrived, when the interests of the Company required that the consideration of its fate in the future should no longer be deferred.

The measures taken by Mr. Crawford are best told in his own words; he says:—

"As a first step I proceeded to prepare a paper, which dealing with some of the leading facts as they lay before us, would familiarise my own mind, and the minds of my colleagues on the Board, and of any other persons under whose observation they might come, with the main features of the case and the magnitude of the interests concerned; at the same time they presented something like a definite proposition for consideration.

"My next step was to write to Lord Salisbury under date 8th March 1877, to the effect that 'as the time approached when the relations of the East Indian Railway Company with the Government of India would come under review in the terms of the contract, we found our freedom of proceeding in the management of the line, and consideration of measures for the development of the traffic, much affected by the uncertainties of our position; requesting in conclusion that His Lordship would allow me to see him on the subject. I waited on him on the 15th March 1877. He heard what I had to say, and having spoken amongst other things of difficulties in the interpretation of the contract, referred me in the end to General Strachey, the Chairman of the Railway Committee of his Council."

"Various communications having passed between General Strachey and myself, I received from him in the result, a declaration of Lord Salisbury's views in the following confidential letter dated 3rd May 1877 :—

"I return the paper you left with me. Acting on your authority to do so, if I thought fit, I have shewed it to Lord Salisbury. To take up the discussion where we left it, I now wish to repeat what I before said, that the only basis on which I have any authority to treat is, that the Railway shall become the property of the State. At the same time it is suggested, that arrangements might be come to between the Government and the Company, under which the Company, either as now constituted or in some modified shape, might continue to work the Railway on a lease for a term of years.

"If no such arrangement commends itself to the Company it will only remain for the Government to act under the terms of the existing contract, when the date for exercising the power of purchase arrives. The exact form that should be given to a working arrangement must be subject of negotiation. The essential condition, which I cannot give up, is, that the prospective share in the profits of the Railway, which a working company shall receive, must be limited to an amount which will fairly represent the remuneration to which they would be entitled for managing the business. I am at present disposed to estimate this as follows :—

"The capital represented by the whole concern being taken at 30 millions, the Government might be expected to share on 25 millions, and would leave 5 millions as the sum on which the Company would share in the division of the profits.

"The five millions in question might be contributed, either as a new subscription of debenture capital, or might be transferred from the amount which the Government will have to pay the Company, as purchase-money, on the termination of the existing contract.

"If such a basis were accepted for discussion, it would, I think, not be difficult to come to an understanding, as to the principles on which the existing shareholders should be paid, on the transfer of the Railway to the Government, so as to give them the full value contemplated by the contract. It would probably simplify matters if this were disposed of quite apart from the arrangement for the future, at least provisionally.

"The question that would then arise would be whether the capital amount, which I have proposed to fix at five millions, should be subscribed as an addition to the existing capital, subject to the condition of being paid up as required from time to time, or whether it should be regarded as having been supplied by a corresponding amount of the sum payable to the shareholders, on the purchase of the Railway by the Government, leaving the future provision of capital to be met independently.

"The net profits to be divided between the Government and the Company would be the net income of the Railway, after deducting the annual sum paid by the Government, in fulfilment of the terms of the old contract and interest on the sum advanced by the Government, as guaranteed, entered with the simple interest accrued thereon, together with all interest on Debentures, not included in the payment under the old contract.

"I think that this includes all the more essential points on which to form an opinion, whether we are likely to come to an understanding as to a working arrangement for the future or the contrary.

"In any case, as Governments are proverbially slow in their action, it has already become time for us to bring our machinery into operation in connection with this question, and if you hear that this has been done, you will not be surprised, though at the same time you are not to assume that there is an intention of closing the door to an arrangement with you, on a basis such as we can accept."

This undoubtedly was a most important communication. It indicated that the Government fully intended to purchase the East Indian Railway, though they did not intend to take it over absolutely, if the Company proved willing to enter into an arrangement for working the line that would meet their views.

Mr. Crawford very carefully considered this letter, and having discussed the terms with his colleagues wrote to General Strachey on the 2nd June, 1877, as follows :—

"I have carefully considered the proposals contained in your letter of the 3rd May. It may suffice for present purposes if I say that they appear to me to contain the basis of a practical working arrangement in the future."

Mr. Crawford in his pamphlet proceeds to say that the whole subject was then, or soon afterwards, submitted for the judgment of the Government of India, and further action on the part of the Board became unnecessary, until, it being made known later on in the autumn that General Strachey was about to go to India, the Board applied for and obtained the sanction of the Government to their Consulting Engineer, Mr. Rendel, proceeding to Calcutta also, in order to facilitate, by his presence on the spot, the settlement of many matters affecting the Railway that were likely to come under discussion.

The reply of the Government of India to the reference of Lord Salisbury having been received, Mr. Crawford was invited by Sir Louis Malet, the Under Secretary of State, on the 16th July, 1878, to call at the India Office, and on doing so found that he had been entrusted by Lord Cranbrook (who had taken the place of Lord Salisbury as Secreary of State) with the negotiations.

Frequent communications followed, in the course of which the whole matter was fully discussed, and ultimately Mr. Crawford met in the room of Sir Louis Mallet at the India Office, Sir John Strachey, the Finance Minister in India, Colonel Williams, the Under Secretary in the Department of Public Works at Calcutta, Mr. Cassells of the Council, Mr. Danvers, the Government Director of Guaranteed Railways, and Mr. Waterfield, the Financial Secretary. This meeting led to still further discussion, and finally an official letter was addressed to Mr. Crawford, as Chairman of the Board, which determined the arrangements subsequently agreed to.

It is unnecessary to trace further the history of these transactions, recorded as they are in the published proceedings of the Company and in the passage of the Bill through Parliament. Nor is it necessary to refer to the measures taken by the Board to carry the provisions of the " Purchase Act" into effect. Enough has been said to shew the course taken up by preliminary negotiations; what followed is too well known to be detailed here.

CHAPTER X.

QUESTIONS BEFORE THE BOARD AFTER THE PURCHASE OF THE RAILWAY BY GOVERNMENT. RETROSPECT OF THE POSITION OF THE COMPANY AT THE TIME—REDUCTION OF THIRD CLASS FARES AND OTHER MATTERS.

ON the last day of the year 1879 the contracts, under which the mutual relations of the Company and the Indian Government had subsisted for more than thirty years, terminated; the undertaking was transferred to the Secretary of State and a fresh agreement for the management and working of the Railway came into force.

The negotiations with the Secretary of State had been long and difficult, but the ultimate arrangement was satisfactory both to the Government and the Company. The real object of the Government in making this new agreement seems to have been to secure to the State a larger share of the profits than it received under the previous contracts, and at the same time to leave the working and management of the line in the hands of the Company who had so successfully administered its affairs in the past.

The general principle of the new contract in regard to the division of earnings was that, having ascertained the amount of net working profits, certain deductions were made in respect of interest charges, contributions to provident fund, and so forth, and the balance, called the surplus profits, was then left to be divided between the Government and the Company in the proportion

4-5ths to Government.
1-5th to the Company.

Now at the time of the purchase of the Railway by the State, the Company had in hand certain surplus assets, amounting to over one hundred thousand pounds, and the question arose how this sum should be disposed of. Part of it consisted of unclaimed interest and dividends and could not be touched, but there remained at the disposal of the shareholders about seventy thousand pounds and out of this it was decided to pay thirty-four thousand to Sir Macdonald Stephenson, in commutation of a pension voted to him some years previously, and from the balance to make a grant to Mr. Robert Ingram Crawford, the Chairman of the Company, whose exceptional services called for some special recognition. Mr. Crawford was one of the few gentlemen who met together, before the East Indian Railway Company was formed, to consider the question whether the railway system was adapted to India and if so how money for the purpose of constructing a railway could best be provided. He and Mr. Stephenson then agreed that nothing could be done without a Government guarantee, but it took them some years to establish the principle of a guarantee, and not until this had been done could the Company be formed. Mr. Crawford had been with the Company from its initiation; he had made himself master of its history and of every one of its transactions; he had been instrumental in introducing many economies and finally had devoted several years of his life to the negotiations with the Government, which had just been brought to a successful issue. It was decided to make him a grant of fifteen thousand pounds, and to divide the balance of the surplus assets among the shareholders.

There were also at this time certain balances at the credit of the "Savings Bank" and "Fine Fund" standing in the books of the Company, apart from the funds of the undertaking, which were also available for disposal.

The position of the subordinate staff of the Company in India, with reference to the education of their children and placing them out in life, had long been an object of solicitude with the Directors, and it was thought that this money might be devoted to the establishment of a school in the hills for the education of the children of Company's servants. The amount available from the combined funds was rather more than four lakhs of rupees and was at least sufficient to form a nucleus for carrying out a scheme of the kind.

Such were among the questions before the Board at the time of the purchase of the Railway by the Government, and we shall hear more about the hill school later on.

The report for the first half of the year 1880 deals for the first time with the undertaking of the East Indian Railway as a whole. Previously the accounts relating to the Main and Jubbulpore lines had been kept separately, but on the first of January 1880, the undertaking was handed over to the Company to be worked without distinction of parts, and consequently the figures, from this time onward, relate to the work done by, and the expenditure and earnings of, the two lines together.

Questions which had been deferred pending settlement of negotiations with the Government as to the future of the Railway now came up for decision. In the new contract the Secretary of State took power to " require the fare of passengers conveyed in closed carriages with seats to be reduced to any rate not below two pies per mile." It will be remembered that the Board had already had under consideration the question of reducing the third class fare, which was then three pies per mile, but although they were not yet prepared to make a definite move, the wishes of Government, as indicated in the contract, were clearly in support of such a measure—what actually followed is described later on.

Then again the report of Mr. Rendel on the subject of his last visit to India had to be dealt with. The chief object of this visit, as already indicated, had been to consider with Mr. Leslie, the Company's Agent at Calcutta, what extension of the works of the Railway, having reference to the then recent rapid increase of traffic, might, on the assumption of its continuance, be necessary within the next few years.

The subject which first engaged Mr. Rendel's attention was one to which the constantly augmenting traffic of the line attached a daily increasing importance, namely, the provision of proper means for transferring goods, on their arrival at Howrah, from the Railway to the ships in the Hooghly river or to warehouses in Calcutta or Howrah and *vice versa*.

The warehouses were mostly on the Calcutta side of the river, and goods leaving the East Indian Railway could only reach them either by being carted over the floating bridge or by boat. A connection by rail was therefore greatly to be desired.

Messrs. Rendel and Leslie now held the opinion that the connection should be made about 24 miles north of Calcutta, thus placing the East Indian Railway in direct communication with the Eastern Bengal Railway and the Port Trust Jetties along the Calcutta fore-shore. The Board accepted their views and the Government after considering the matter proposed that the bridge should be constructed by the East Indian Railway as part of the undertaking.

The cost of the bridge, excluding the sum required for the approaches and for the junction of the two lines, was originally estimated at Rs. 20,00,000 and the Railway Company at once agreed to undertake the work. Mr. Leslie came to England and, in consultation with Mr. A. M. Rendel, drew up designs which were sanctioned shortly afterwards.

In 1880 Dr. Saise, F.G.S., Assistant Manager of the Company's Collieries, made a very careful survey of the coal-fields then opened up in Bengal and summed up his conclusions in the following words :—

"The output of the coal-field is from 400,000 to 450,000 tons per annum, of which the East Indian Railway raises 250,000 to 300,000 tons; assuming an output of 500,000 tons, the coal-field will have a life of 162 years."

The output of the collieries has for many years very largely exceeded Dr. Saise's estimate of 500,000 tons a year, and as far as the East Indian Railway is concerned, its collieries are unable to turn out enough coal to meet its own requirements. The Railway has in consequence to buy part of its supplies in the open market, but then it must not be forgotten that the field of operations has also been greatly extended.

The length of line open in 1880 was 1,504¼ miles, or from Howrah to Delhi with certain branch lines. The total length of railways open to traffic throughout India was at that time 9,148¾ miles, and we find in the administration report a reference to the development of Indian Railways, which illustrates the feeling of Government in those days :—

"The year 1880 is remarkable in the history of railways in India as being connected with three important events. It has seen an unprecedentedly rapid and successful development of State railways, it has witnessed the introduction of private enterprise into railway construction, it marks the date of the railway conference."

The battle of the gauges had only just been determined and railway competition had, compared with present day competition, hardly begun. Still in the Traffic Manager's report for the second half of the year a reference is made to competition; speaking of the speed of goods trains the remark appears :—

"It behoves us now that Railway Companies are competing with us so keenly, to increase as far as possible the speed of goods trains;" and again—"It is much to be regretted that our new engines cannot be run at a higher speed than 13 and 15 miles an hour with 600 ton loads."

The head-quarters of the Traffic Department were at Jamalpur, Mr. N. St. Leger Carter was the Traffic Manager, he had with him a Deputy and a Personal Assistant and the line was divided into five Traffic Districts. Some idea of the working may be derived from a glance at the time tables and goods and coaching tariffs of the period.

The Chord line mail train used to leave Howrah at 9 P.M., Calcutta time, it reached Dinapore at 10-25 the next morning, Allahabad at 7-8 P.M., halted at Cawnpore from 1-20 to 1-50 A.M. and arrived at Delhi at 2-45 P.M., on the second day, thus taking $42\frac{1}{4}$ hours between Howrah and Delhi, a through speed of little more than $22\frac{1}{2}$ miles an hour. The load was 16 vehicles and no third class passengers were carried below Allahabad; the parcels and luggage traffic was nominal, so that it is hard to find any justification for what appear to have been most unnecessarily long halts all along the route. That at Cawnpore, in the middle of the night, could only have been allowed with the object of regaining time lost elsewhere.

The down mail did the same run in practically the same time as the up, and besides the mail trains there was but one through passenger train each way, which took over 53 hours to cover the 954 miles.

A second passenger train terminated at Allahabad, a mail and a passenger train ran between Howrah and Burdwan, and a few locals for a shorter distance, between Howrah and Pundooah. The load of these local trains was 20 vehicles.

The number of stations open for traffic was naturally far less than now, some of the runs on the Howrah district being as long as 12 miles, while on the Upper Districts this was the ordinary distance between stations and some runs were far longer, as much in fact as 16¼ miles.

The Coaching tariff, then called the Time and Fare Table, was a small volume of 78 pages and contained train timings, fares and rules. The intermediate class fare was 4½ pies per mile, and the third class 3 pies, but as has been already indicated, the question of reducing the latter was under consideration. The Traffic Manager held the opinion that reduction was unnecessary, and his opinion was shared by other officials in India. Naturally, the question was one for considerable controversy. There were two proposals, one to reduce the fare from 3 to 2½ pies per mile, the other to reduce to 2 pies. Both proposals were strenuously opposed by the Agent, the Traffic Manager and Chief Auditor, mainly on the ground that if either of them had the anticipated effect of increasing abnormally, the number of passengers to be carried, the provision of sufficient vehicles in which to carry them would become an impossibility! In spite of this opposition, the reduction to 2½ pies, ordered by Government as an experimental measure, was supported by the Home Board, who indeed had no alternative but to acquiesce, although they were admittedly doubtful as to the expediency of the move. The reduced fare was introduced on the Jubbulpore branch and on the main line above Naini in January 1882, being extended below Naini in July following.

The earnings from third class passengers at once responded; in 1881 they amounted to Rs. 90,02,162, in 1882 they went up to Rs. 99,99,999. It is only fair to mention that this great rise in the earnings was partly due to a Kumbh Mela at Allahabad, still there was never, in after years, any loss in a year's figures; on the contrary the third class traffic continued to respond and the lesson of the reduction is one to be remembered. To illustrate how strenuously it was opposed in India, the following extract from the Traffic Manager's report for the first half of 1881 will suffice :—

"Third class passengers as usual shew a decided increase on the figures of any previous half year, rendering still more incomprehensible and inexplicable the course to be pursued of reducing the third class fare by one-sixth."

Successive half-yearly reports harped on the question, but the only explanation can be that previous remarks had in some way or another to be justified; thus we find that in the second half-year of 1882, a temporary falling off in intermediate class passengers is attributed to the reduction in third class fares, and again in 1884, it was actually proposed that the old fares should be reverted to, the Traffic Manager writing :—

"It is evident from the low average distance travelled by third class passengers, that the reduction made in 1882 in the hope of encouraging longer journeys has entirely failed in its object, and I think the time has now arrived to revert to our former rate of 3 pies per mile for the greater portion of the line."

So much for the controversy on third class passenger fares, the reduction was evidently a very sore point, but the results proved from the outset that it was fully justified. Since those days the average distance travelled by each passenger has become still shorter, but this is due, not to reduction in fares, but to the greater number of people who have gradually been induced to take the rail for short journeys, instead of walking the distance, and also to the opening of alternative routes.

The fares for first and second class passengers were much the same in 1880 as at the present time, first class one anna and-a-half and second class nine pies, but no reduction was then made, as it is now, for long distance journeys. Efforts were however being considered to develop the higher classes, and we read as a novel feature in Indian Railway administration, of the opening of negotiations with Messrs. Thos. Cook & Son, the well-known tourist agents. In the year 1880, Messrs. Thos. Cook & Son started their first agency in India at Bombay.

The goods and mineral traffic was contending with what we would now consider a very high tariff. Giridih coal worth Rs. 3 a ton in wagons at the Collieries, cost Rs. 30 a ton by the time it reached Lahore, while to Calcutta the freight charge from Sitarampur was no less than Rs. 3-13 a ton. No rebates whatever were allowed and with such a tariff in force there is no wonder that English coal readily found its way to Calcutta. The Traffic Manager in his report for the second half of the year 1880 remarks :—

"During the first three months of the half year there was a brisk traffic in coal to the Port, but in October and subsequently, owing to large arrivals of foreign coal brought by steamers and ships as ballast, the demand for Indian coal considerably abated."

The quantity of English coal imported into India in the year was no less than 683,768 tons. Madras found it cheaper to use patent fuel brought from England than to depend on Indian coal. The total weight of coal despatched downwards in the year 1880 was 563,241 tons; since then we have seen in a single year a downwards coal traffic of 4,881,524 tons.

But though the downwards coal traffic was so poor, the upwards was still poorer; the upwards figures for the year being 168,990 tons against an upwards traffic in the year 1905 of 1,260,740 tons. Efforts were however being made to develop a better traffic with the railways and mills in Upper India. In October 1880 the charge for coal in full wagon loads, carried not less than 300 miles, was reduced from $\frac{1}{5}$th to $\frac{1}{6}$th pie per maund per mile. It was hoped at the time that this reduction would enable up-country mills to use coal in place of wood fuel.

But it was not only the coal rates that required reducing, the coal-fields of Bengal, as we now know them, were scarcely touched and the assistance given to colliery proprietors was nominal. It was recorded at the time, as a great concession, that with a view to the encouragement of trade, the Railway Company would lend second-hand rails to those who could not meet the entire cost of providing themselves with the necessary sidings to their pits, and in 1881 the Company discontinued the sale of coal to outsiders.

Apart from coal, the rates for all classes of merchandise were exceedingly high compared with what they now are, and in some instances transport difficulties were enormous. As an instance the route from Calcutta to Darjeeling was *viâ* Sahebgunge. Goods were forwarded by rail to Sahebgunge, thence by steam ferry across the Ganges to a place called Caragola and onward by bullock cart. The charge for tea from Darjeeling, where by the way the East Indian Railway had an out-agency, to Caragola, was over Rs. 2-0-0 per maund, and for salt in the upwards direction nearly Rs. 3-0-0, and yet the traffic was growing.

The rate for wheat from Delhi to Howrah was 13 annas per maund compared with 0-7-11 per maund, the present rate. The whole of the goods tariff was contained in one small volume; now the goods tariff comprises three large volumes, and there is a separate one for coal. The total goods earnings of the year were well under 300 lacs of rupees or less than a poor half year's earnings now.

But great changes were coming on apace. Up to 1881 Calcutta was much in advance of Bombay in the quantity of wheat and seeds exported from India, while Kurrachee was a port of minor significance. The opening up of a large wheat-producing country, by the construction of the Rajputana Railway, altered the aspect entirely, for in addition to opening up a new country, this Railway also had the effect of directly connecting the Punjab with Bombay ; and although Calcutta still continued to do well in seeds, Bombay shot ahead with its wheat exports and following this the source of wheat supply gradually moved from Bengal to the North-West.

The opening up of the Rajputana Railway shortened the distance between Delhi and Bombay by 345 miles and distances now compared :—

	Miles.
Bombay to Delhi *viâ* Bombay, Baroda and Central India and Rajputana Railway	889
Ditto. *viâ* Jubbulpore	1,234
Ditto Calcutta to Delhi	954

As a consequence the question of competition between Bombay and Calcutta assumed what was described as " a position of grave importance," and so much consideration had to be given to it that Mr. Leslie, the Agent and Chief Engineer, was relieved of his duties as Chief Engineer, retaining only charge of the Hooghly bridge, and Mr. C. H.

Denham was appointed Chief Engineer. This question of competition between Bombay and Calcutta is dealt with however in greater detail elsewhere.

In spite of all this the first half of the year 1883 will long be remembered by those who were on the line at the time as a record wheat year. The Howrah sheds were blocked for weeks, with the grain which came from Cawnpore, Benares, Patna and other points, and the resources of the Railway to carry it were taxed to the utmost. Mr. Urban Broughton, who was officiating Traffic Manager, devised a system of night deliveries from Howrah passenger station, and even third class carriages were requisitioned to load the grain when wagons could not be got. As a climax the water-supply on the Chord line failed and much of the traffic had to be diverted over the single line *viâ* the loop. Fortunately this did not occur until the month of June, by when the great bulk of the traffic had already passed down and the rains were near at hand.

In these days the earnings from wheat were often heavier than from coal; in the first half of 1883 the freight earned on the wheat carried was over 31 lacs of rupees, whereas from coal the takings were under 30 lacs.

The wheat traffic of 1883 was the heaviest ever carried until 1904. The figures of these two years are interesting as indicating, not only the great increase in weight carried in the latter period, but the reduction in freight earned owing to the heavy reductions in rates charged.

	Tons.	Rs.
1883	... 469,173	53,76,535
1904	... 759,162	48,46,310

Some attention was given in the early eighties to the question of train loads, the loads of goods trains above Moghalsarai were raised from 400 to 450 tons and below Asansol from 600 to 700 tons. But although these loads were permissible it is not evident that measures were taken to ensure their being availed of, as the average load of goods trains was not more than 175 tons.

With the sanction of Government new Provident Fund rules were introduced in 1881. Under these rules, though the main principles of the original fund were upheld, certain important modifications were introduced. A distinction which previously existed between Europeans and non-Europeans was abolished, all servants of the Company, without distinction of race, drawing Rs. 15 per mensem and above, were called upon to subscribe 5 per cent. of their pay to the Fund and each member was given the option of subscribing an additional amount not exceeding another 5 per cent. It was laid down that the contribution of the undertaking would be declared on the net profits of the year only, and that no *ad interim* contribution would be made in respect of the first half of the year as had hitherto been done. These rules continued in force until 1903 when, as shewn in another chapter, they were further modified and the existing rules introduced.

CHAPTER XI.

GROWTH OF THE COAL TRADE IN 1883—THE QUESTION OF WORKING THE EAST INDIAN RAILWAY BY STATE OR COMPANY MANAGEMENT—AGITATION IN CALCUTTA REGARDING CONSTRUCTION OF THE GRAND CHORD.—RETIREMENT OF SIR BRADFORD LESLIE.—DEATH OF MR. CRAWFORD.

FOLLOWING the great wheat export trade of 1883, there was a short period of depression. In 1883 everything had been in favour of the exportation of Indian wheat; the stocks held in England and on the Continent were small and there were poor harvests, both in Europe and America. But in 1884 the position was reversed and the average price of wheat in England became lower than it had been since the year 1780. During the first half of 1884 there was, on the East Indian Railway, a decrease in wheat traffic alone of no less than 158,084 tons, and the only considerable set off was an increase of 53,785 tons in the weight of coal carried.

The coal trade which for some years had been slowly developing, was now beginning to attract attention. When the East Indian Railway was constructed, coal was almost unknown in India. Mr. Crawford referring to this in 1885, remarked :—

"If a man fell in with a bit of coal in his walk, he would pick it up as a curiosity, and throw it away because it dirtied his finger. That was all that was known of coal 30 years ago. It was the act of this Company which brought coal to light. From a basis of comparatively nothing 30 years ago, we have now risen to carry one million and a half tons in the course of the year. The native mind is so full of prejudice, that one might have been afraid that the use of an article like coal would have excited some superstitious feeling, but when the native came to know that coal was only fossilized wood, he had no objection to burn it, and with such an enormous population as we have in India, with such large cities and factories rising in all quarters and steam engines and so on, we see the explanation of the great increase in the quantity of coal brought to us for conveyance. So it will go on and very largely increase. I venture to predict that the time will come, which I shall probably not witness, when the article of coal will be our largest source of profit."

Mr. Crawford had great foresight and his prediction has come true, but he seems to have looked more to the internal consumption of coal than to the export trade, which has been where the largest growth has actually come. The natives of India have not yet taken freely to the use of coal as fuel for domestic purposes, when they do so the consumption will be enormous; and it is perfectly certain that sooner or later the time must arrive when they will have to, for wood fuel and charcoal are becoming more and more scarce every year, and there is nothing left to burn, but dried cowdung or coal. Already we find coal used by natives for brick burning and for manufacturing purposes. Sweetmeat makers use it and it is burnt by blacksmiths even in remote villages, but for cooking purposes, or for heating houses in the cold season, or for other similar domestic use, we very seldom see coal burnt, except perhaps in the vicinity of the colliery district or in Calcutta and the neighbourhood. The retail price is in fact still too high to suit the pockets of the majority.

In the year 1884, in the course of an enquiry before a select Committee of the House of Commons on " East India Railway Communications," Mr. Juland Danvers, the then Government Director of Guaranteed Railway Companies and Secretary in the Public Works Department at the India Office, being asked to state his reasons for an opinion he had given, that he thought that the Agency of both the State and of private enterprise might usefully be employed in working railways in India, though, as a principle, he preferred that of companies, replied :—

"The advantages of making use of private enterprise, even when assisted by guarantees or subsidies, appear to me to be these. It relieves an already overburdened Government of duties which can be equally well performed by others. It prevents an increase to Government establishments and to pension lists. It secures more steady progress, by avoiding interruptions to which State undertakings are liable. It secures also the supply of money as required, and its application to the special purpose which an arrangement between the Government and the company is intended to fulfil, whereas war, famine, and other exigencies of State may interfere with the supply of money when most required for works under Government. It avoids the disadvantages appertaining to State agency, which is liable, more or less, according to circumstances and to the character of those in authority, to be affected by influences from which a company under proper State and legislative supervision is free. It ensures better than any other way the formation of railway systems or administrations of suitable size. It is the best way of securing a healthy competition. Supposing a system of Government agency to be carried out in its entirety, a huge state monopoly would be established which would not be advantageous to the country or conducive to the interests of the various districts traversed. Upon the whole, therefore, I think that, under suitable legislative enactments, and with fair competition, the best results will be secured by employing companies as far as practicable. Might I be allowed to quote a high authority in support of this view, namely, Lord Salisbury. When he was Secretary of State he had to consider the question of purchasing the East Indian Railway and in a despatch to the Government of India relating to that proposition he says :—

'The question is shall the Railway, if purchased by the Government, be worked directly by the State, or shall an attempt be made to continue the working through the agency of a company, suitably constituted, to which the Railway shall be leased for a term of years? I am not disposed to call in question the possibility of carrying out the working of a railway, such as the East Indian, through Government agency in a satisfactory manner. But the difficulties in the way of combining the habitual, and indeed necessary rigidity, with which a system of Government financial and administrative control must work, with the freedom of action required for the successful management of a constantly varying business like that of a railway, made up of a vast mass of details, would be considerable; and to avoid them would require both a happy selection of officers and well-contrived administrative rules and methods, which, though no doubt attainable, could not be confidently or permanently reckoned upon. I view with no small anxiety the ever continued expansion of the vast establishments of your Government, which, as they grow, place an ever increasing weight of business on yourself and your officers, whose strength is already over-taxed, and leave an ever diminishing area for independent action. That such a state of things is, to some extent, an almost necessary consequence of our position in India, may be true; but this in itself is an argument for resisting the tendency, when it may be done without the sacrifice of objects of evident importance. For such reasons I should in the present case, as now advised, gladly hear from Your Excellency's Government that you were of opinion that the working of the East Indian Railway might, without objection, be entrusted to a private company, in the event of the purchase of the line being effected.'

"The result we know. The working arrangement was made, and I think it will be admitted that the best results have ensued."

Mr. Danvers strongly advocated the policy of employing private enterprise and experience, in opposition to State line management, and Mr. Crawford in 1885 wrote a brochure or pamphlet called "The Result we know," the object of which was, by an analysis of statistics for the preceding five years, to verify the truth upon which Mr. Danvers' argument was founded, and to place on record what private experience and private direction had effected, in the case of the East Indian Railway.

It is unnecessary to quote in detail from this brochure, but as a result of the examination of the figures relating to the coaching and goods traffic, the Board of Directors wrote several letters to the Agent in India, impressing upon him the necessity of examining into and cultivating every possible means of increasing the traffic of the line. Particular stress was laid on the desirability of developing the local movement of passengers and goods, by reducing charges and affording facilities between large internal centres, and by encouraging the use of coal for domestic purposes. The letters in fact were a clear indication of the liberal intentions of the Board and a guide to the policy they desired should generally be followed.

During the next few years the competition between Bombay and Calcutta became more acute and considerable reductions were made in the railway rates, by the different administrations interested. At about the same time some correspondence arose as to the construction of the Grand Chord line, attempts being made to influence public opinion towards its being carried out by the Oudh and Rohilkhand Railway, but the claim of the East Indian was beyond dispute and nothing came of the agitation.

One of Mr. Crawford's last acts as Chairman of the East Indian Railway Company was to publish "some observations on the remarks of Sir Alexander Wilson at the Annual General Meeting of the Bengal Chamber of Commerce on the 28th February 1889 and other sayings and doings at Calcutta in connection with the proposed Grand Chord line."

The President of the Chamber of Commerce had said at the Annual Meeting held in Calcutta on the 28th February, 1889, that the East Indian Railway was the sole means of transport between the North-West Provinces and Calcutta; that its resources were inadequate for the trade of the country;

that it maintained a high tariff of rates and only granted concessions when competition necessitated its doing so; that trade was gradually being deflected from Calcutta and that an independent alternative route was necessary, in order to break down the monopoly possessed by the East Indian Railway.

On all these points Mr. Crawford had observations to make and in addition reprinted a letter from X. B. E. which had appeared in the *Englishman* of the 13th March, 1889. This letter afforded a most complete answer to the statements put forward at the meeting of the Chamber of Commerce, and Mr. Crawford had but little to add to it. The writer, who it is not difficult to identify, was even as long ago as 1889, one of the best-known railway men in India. The letter was as follows :—

Sir,
    I have read with much interest the remarks made by the President at the recent annual meeting of the Bengal Chamber of Commerce, on the subject of the extension and development of the railway system in India, and more particularly the construction of a second line of railway between the North-West Provinces and the port of Calcutta. The President had come to the conclusion and the Hon. Mr. Steel considered Sir A. Wilson's remarks worthy of profound enquiry and deliberation, that a second railway under management independent of the East Indian Railway was really required, on the following grounds :—

    1. That it has been seen over and over again, when there have been times of pressure, how inadequate the resources of the East Indian Railway have been for the requirements of the State and the trade of the country.

    2. That the East Indian Railway being a monopolist company, a high tariff of rates has been maintained, from which concessions have been so grudgingly extracted that

Calcutta merchants have seen their trade gradually but steadily deflecting to the other side of India, and under existing circumstances have been powerless to stop this deflection.

3. That the competition resulting from the construction of an alternative route would ensure proper accommodation for goods and traffic and bring down rates sufficiently, to attract again to Calcutta, a considerable amount of the traffic which is now attracted by cheaper land carriage to the Western Coast.

4 That competition alone will secure that control of rates so essential to the development of the resources of the country and that all control over the East Indian Railway rates has been abandoned by Government.

If you will permit me to remark, under each of these four heads, I shall be much obliged.

The line stated to be necessary is that affording an alternative route between Moghalsarai and Calcutta.

1. The statement that the East Indian Railway has repeatedly failed in times of pressure seems rather sweeping. It is extremely questionable whether it can be stated that the capacity of this Railway to transport traffic over its lines between stations has ever been approached. There is a double line throughout between Moghalsarai and Howrah, and the only means of ascertaining whether more lines of rails are required seems to be to determine what daily tonnage can be hauled over the present lines, and what tonnage could be given by Calcutta merchants, with favourable rates to Calcutta, as compared with the charges to Western Ports, taken advantage of by Calcutta. If it be found that the double line of the East Indian Railway Company is prepared to deal with a considerable progressive development of traffic, why should money be sunk in 400 or more miles of new line, if the alternative railway is intended to enter Calcutta at a separate terminus from that of the East Indian Railway, as would appear to be the intention of the President of the Chamber of Commerce ? The difficulties referred to by the President have, even in the merchants' view, been practically confined to terminal accommodation. The only serious difficulty was in 1883, when export trade developed suddenly beyond all expectations. Merchants had neither cargo, boats nor carts to clear arrivals to their full extent ; no steamers, nor warehouses in which to stow consignments when cleared, the result being that the then existing

accommodation at Howrah became "congested" and eventually rolling stock, instead of transporting grain and seeds, became locked up in warehousing them at Howrah. Since 1883 the railway accommodation has been largely increased, and only three years later, in 1886, Howrah dealt with the same weight of traffic in the busy months as in 1883, without difficulties either to merchants or the railway. Since 1886 the shed room at Howrah has been further increased, and there is now also the option to merchants to deliver on the Calcutta side.

2. If the East Indian Railway is a monopolist company, it must be admitted that it uses its powers with great consideration towards its constituents. The Administration Report recently issued by the Director-General of Railways shews that the charges levied by certain railways for the carriage of goods vary as below:—

Average sum in pies received for carrying a ton of goods one mile :—

East Indian.	North Western.	Great Indian Peninsular.	Baroda	Rajputana.
5·96	6·43	8·21	9·19	8·08

The charges by the East Indian Railway are, therefore much lower than those of the lines serving Bombay and Kurrachee. In other words Calcutta has an immense advantage over Bombay in the matter of railway charges.

3. As explained under head (1) it is very much open to question, indeed, whether Calcutta, including Howrah, has not ample accommodation for the present, and even for a largely increased trade. On the other hand, there seems to have been no attempt to show that a new line, running, as must the alternative route, through a country already served by the East Indian Railway and branches, can attract any considerable new traffic. If the two railways were under separate managements, and proceeded to competition, the undoubtedly low rates already charged by the East Indian would be liable to further reduction, and there would be every probability of the new railway becoming a burden to its owners. There is only one railway in India charging lower rates than the East Indian, and that railway, although open for a number of years, returns only 3¼ per cent. per annum on the capital outlay. As regards

the alleged cheaper land carriage to Bombay, the President was clearly in error in his statement on this point. The distance from Calcutta to Bombay, *viâ* Jubbulpore, is 1,400 miles, Jubbulpore being distant 616 miles from Bombay and 784 miles from Calcutta. Even at Jubbulpore and at the important station of Sihora, near to Jubbulpore, charges are greatly in favour of Calcutta, notwithstanding the shortest lead to Bombay, while from Kirwee 673 miles from Bombay and 727 miles from Calcutta, the charges for grain and seeds are, per hundred maunds—

	Rs.	As.	P.
To Bombay ...	69	6	0
To Calcutta ...	50	0	0

4. The question whether the control of rates has been abandoned by Government appears to be one requiring the confirmation of Government or of the East Indian Railway. It is to the mutual interests of Calcutta merchants and of the East Indian Railway to keep trade to Calcutta and prevent diversion to Western Ports, and all will agree that the East Indian Railway must be reasonable in its charges, when the fact is known that last year Bombay got the lion's share of the trade from an important station, distant 540 miles from Calcutta and 880 miles from Bombay, rates Rs. 43 per hundred maunds in favour of Calcutta. In other words the charge to Bombay was almost twice as much as to Calcutta.

All circumstances considered, it is submitted that further enquiry on the part of the Chamber is desirable regarding the facilities they already receive from the existing line of communication.

X. B. E.

To this letter no convincing reply was forthcoming, but after many years the Government, as will be seen in another chapter, sanctioned the construction of the Grand Chord line as part of the undertaking of the East Indian Railway.

It need hardly be pointed out that the interests of the State and of the East Indian

Railway Company are, and always have been, identical, and both would have been seriously affected by a diminution of the traffic of the Main Line, had the construction of the Grand Chord Line been entrusted to a rival company. And it is difficult to see that the public would in any way have benefited.

The development of the Bengal and North Western Railway led to the opening of the Digha Ghât branch, where it was intended that the bulk of the traffic between that system and the East Indian Railway should be interchanged by means of a steam ferry, for the conveyance of wagons across the river Ganges.

The Tarkessur Railway, constructed by private enterprise, was handed over to the East Indian Railway to work on the 1st January, 1885, and in the same year the Indian Midland Railway was formed under the auspices of the Great Indian Peninsular, with the object of connecting that system with the East Indian Railway at Cawnpore and Agra. The Hooghly Bridge was completed and formally opened to traffic by His Excellency the Viceroy on the 21st February, 1887, receiving from him the appropriate name of the "Jubilee Bridge," while Sir Bradford Leslie, its constructor, was appointed a Knight Commander of the Indian Empire. The bridge over the Ganges at Benares was also completed in 1887, and in the same year the distinction of Knight

Commander of the Indian Empire was conferred on Sir Alexander M. Rendel, who had then been for upwards of thirty years the Consulting Engineer of the Company.

Sir Bradford Leslie, K.C.I.E., retired in 1887, and was succeeded as Agent by Mr. David Wilkinson Campbell, C I.E., who was at the time the Locomotive Superintendent of the Company. Shortly after his retirement Sir Bradford Leslie put forward a scheme for the construction of a new line of railway, between Moghalsarai and the town of Hooghly, to compete with the East Indian Railway. The Board lost no time in entering with the Secretary of State their protest against this scheme, on the ground "that the construction by this Company of a Grand Chord line between Sitarampur and Moghalsarai, the main line originally proposed and surveyed by this Company in 1850, would be the natural complement to a line following the course of the Ganges, whenever the circumstances of the country, commercial, political or otherwise, should require it and justify the large expenditure which it would involve."

In 1888 the first portion of the Company's hill school at Mussoorie was opened. This school which has since proved a great benefit to the Company's employés, is not intended for the education of the children of servants of the superior grade but for the children of those who, by reason of their position in the service, lack the means of sending them to be educated in England. A more detailed account of the Hill School will be found elsewhere.

In 1888 Sir Macdonald Stephenson resigned his position as Deputy Chairman of the Board, though he continued on the directorate until 1892, and in 1889 Mr. Crawford, who for thirty-five years had been Chairman of the Company, died. These two had been associated in the formation of the Company, Mr. Crawford had been a Director as early as 1847 and had been Chairman of the Board since 1854. His services both in the interests of Government and in those of the shareholders had been of a specially valuable nature.

Mr. Crawford, to quote from Herepath, "had a great eye for figures"; like all masters of the arithmetical and statistical craft, he put life and force into his statistics; giving them that margin which never fails to carry home the particular point to be inculcated.

CHAPTER XII.

Appointment of General Sir Richard Strachey as Chairman—His visit to India.

On the 10th of October, 1889, General Strachey was appointed Chairman of the Board of Directors, and immediately decided upon a personal visit to India. Accompanied by Sir Alexander Rendel, the Consulting Engineer of the Company, he sailed in January and arrived in Bombay on the 1st February, 1890.

General Strachey remained in India until the middle of March, and during his six weeks' stay dealt with many important questions. He instituted an enquiry into the routine of the Company's work, by appointing a committee to investigate the manner in which all departments were conducted; the general object being to simplify procedure and expedite the transaction of business without impairing efficiency. He gave his attention to the train service, and particularly to the transit of goods, directing that immediate steps should be taken to improve the speed of trains, and that "at all events one despatch shall be provided to carry goods of the higher class directly to Cawnpore," for in those days there was no direct service between Calcutta and

Photo. by Fredk. Hollyer.

LIEUT.-GENL. SIR RICHARD STRACHEY, R.E.,
G.C.S.I., LL.D., F.R.S., F.R.G.S.

CHAIRMAN, EAST INDIAN RAILWAY.

Cawnpore, and merchants complained bitterly of the unconscionable time their consignments took in transit. He arranged for sanction to the sinking of trial pits to test the quality of coal in the Jherriah coal-field, with a view to the opening up of that field by extending the Barrakur branch line, which then terminated at Barrakur, across the river. He attended meetings of the Chamber of Commerce, both in Calcutta and Cawnpore, and originated the idea of a local Consultative Board. He studied the question of coal rates, and modified the terms under which sidings to mills and collieries were constructed, so as to make them less burdensome than they then were. He re-opened the question of constructing the Grand Chord line, and of putting in additional branch lines as feeders to the main line; reviewed the position in regard to the opening of the Kidderpore Docks, and dealt with numerous other important issues under consideration at the time. This visit of the Chairman to India was in fact attended with far reaching results, but above all, it gave the Government of India, the servants of the Railway Company, and the public who were its constituents, a very clear indication of what his future policy would be. It was at once recognised that a new *régime* had set in, and that, as General Strachey remarked at the time, " with the advance of knowledge and experience many changes had become desirable which should not be deferred."

In 1889, the Head-Quarters of the Traffic Department were at Jamalpur, an out-of-the-way station on the loop line, where for months together a merchant was never seen. One of the first acts of the Home Board, after the appointment of General Strachey as Chairman, was to direct that the Traffic Manager should make Calcutta his future Head-Quarters, so that he might "be more in touch with the merchants and traders of Calcutta than is now possible, distant, as he is, some 300 miles from the port." The move was not a popular one with the Traffic Department, and many arguments were advanced against it, but the wisdom of the change soon became apparent and was naturally insisted upon. One can hardly conceive now how the traffic business of the undertaking could be managed from any other place than Calcutta, where the Head of the Department is not only in constant touch with the mercantile community, but is in the same building as the Agent, the Chief Engineer, the Chief Auditor and other officials of the Company, and of the Government, thus effecting a great economy in time and correspondence.

It was in 1889 that the enormous possibilities of a development of the coal trade first attracted serious attention. Steamer companies trading to the East were beginning to realize the advantage of utilising local sources of supply, instead of importing

Welsh coal to Indian ports; the rapid extension of Indian railways opened up a growing field for the consumption of Bengal coal, while mills and factories realized that their requirements were only limited by the excessive railway freight charged.

The British India Steam Navigation Company, having large interests in sea-going steamers, represented that they were anxious to establish, at several ports, depôts of Bengal coal, in replacement of the Welsh coal they had previously used. The Government was anxious to secure more favourable rates for the carriage of coal for the consumption of State railways, and, in fact, claimed that all such coal should be charged at the minimum permissible rate. Simultaneously with this, the mill-owners of Cawnpore were agitating for better terms for the transport of their coal, while other influential people were advocating the expediency of reducing the rates on the cheaper classes of fuel, in view of the probable development of brick burning. Certain concessions were at once made, a rebate of 16 per cent. on the then tariff was granted on exported coal, and a rebate of 10 per cent. on rubble or slack coal. But General Strachey recognised that it was no time for half measures: it was evident to him that the whole question would have to be very carefully considered, and his policy became clear, when, during his visit, he declined to agree with the Government claim that coal for the use of State Railways should be carried at a lower rate than coal for other railways, or, in fact, that there should be any differentiation between rates allowed to any particular class of consumers.

This question of coal rates was indeed one of the most important subjects raised during the Chairman's visit to India, and, although no immediate settlement was then come to, beyond the settlement of certain general principles, still the basis was laid for the consideration of the coal tariff as a whole, and this, coupled with the projected opening up of the Jherriah coalfield, and of the Kidderpore Docks, laid the foundation for the enormous traffic since developed.

CHAPTER XIII.

THE GRAND CHORD LINE.

THE question of constructing what is known as the Grand Chord Line, long advocated by Mr. Crawford, was one of the subjects put before General Strachey during his visit to India. The Grand Chord Line had first been surveyed in 1850, with the idea of constructing the original main line by that route, it being the more direct way to the North-West; but the Government of the day preferred, and no doubt wisely preferred, the somewhat more circuitous Loop Line route, which tapped the great cities and trade centres along the banks of the River Ganges. Mr. Crawford in 1886 reopened the question of constructing the Grand Chord, on the ground that it would not only form a relief to the growing traffic of the main line, but would consolidate the great railway system of the Gangetic Valley. Without going into the earlier history of the project it is enough to say here that, before the arrival of General Strachey, the country had been re-surveyed by Mr. Parker, one of the Company's Engineers, and that estimates of the cost of construction had been prepared, which included a branch to the Palamow coal-field and a branch into Jherriah, though it was admitted that the precise location of the different lines comprising the scheme might eventually be altered and improved. General Strachey directed that the estimates should be placed before the Government of India, with an offer to construct both the Grand Chord Line and the branches referred to as part of the undertaking. This was in the early part of 1890.

Years passed and nothing could be done owing to the impossibility of obtaining the requisite funds, but at last, in 1895, the Government authorised part of the work being begun, under certain specified conditions, which the Board accepted. In the meantime, as detailed elsewhere, there had been considerable discussion as to the agency through which the Grand Chord Line should be constructed, and it was a subject for congratulation that the just claims of the East Indian Railway were not passed over. General Strachey in advising the shareholders of the decision remarked : " I need not therefore dwell on this subject beyond expressing my satisfaction that the question, as to the Company being eventually placed in a position to carry out the Grand Chord Line, is now virtually settled and that no further controversy regarding it will be possible. I may, however, take the opportunity of adding that the

Board, and I feel sure you will all agree with them, while consistently holding the opinion that the Company was fairly entitled to construct the Grand Chord Line, as a part of the undertaking of the East Indian Railway, when circumstances were held to be ripe for it and that its eventual construction was inevitable, as it offered the shortest possible route between the Upper Provinces and Calcutta, yet have never made objections to opening up a fresh route giving access to Calcutta."

The first portion of the line to be constructed was the section from Gya to Moghalsarai, including the important bridge over the Soane River at Dehree and the branch to the Palamow coal-fields. After this portion had been opened for traffic, the Government accorded sanction to the construction of the remaining portion, between Gya and the Barrakur branch; this latter section, which involves very heavy work through a hilly country, is now nearing completion and should be opened for traffic before the close of 1906.

The construction of the Grand Chord Line will shorten the distance between the Upper Provinces of India and Calcutta by 50 miles and will bring the Jherriah coal-fields much nearer to these Provinces. Its opening will not only cheapen coal in Upper India, but will involve a reduction in the charges for transport of a considerable proportion of the traffic now carried to and from stations above Moghalsarai. How far such reduction in charge will be followed by increased traffic remains to be seen, but there is little doubt that the opening of a shorter route will be of some benefit to the port of Calcutta in its competition with Bombay, and although, judging by the nature of the country traversed by a considerable portion of the new line, it is doubtful whether its local traffic will prove more than nominal, there is no reason to look forward to the result with any anxiety.

CHAPTER XIV.

THE JHERRIAH COAL-FIELD.

As early as 1886 proposals were made by the Railway Company to construct a bridge across the river at Barrakur, and to extend the branch line, which then terminated at that station, to the collieries on the other side. In other words the Company had long recognised that a bridge over the Barrakur River was the key to the Jherriah field.

Some time before General Strachey visited India in 1899, Mr. Ward, Manager of the Company's Collieries, had made a preliminary survey of this coal-field, which lay still further inland than the collieries immediately beyond the Barrakur River, which the railway first intended to serve. The results of this survey were thought sufficiently satisfactory to induce the Chairman, during his stay in India, to solicit the approval of the Government of India to the sinking of trial pits to test the quality of the coal; while the question of extending the Barrakur branch line into Jherriah was at the same time mooted.

In 1890 a further report on the Jherriah field was submitted by Mr. Ward. This report established beyond question that the area surveyed contained a coal-field of very great extent, both in respect to the quality of coal and its value.

Estimates and plans of a projected line of railway from Barrakur Station to the Jherriah coal-field, a distance of about 36 miles, were prepared, and the Board sanctioned the estimates subject to the confirmation of the Government of India. With a view to expediting matters the Board also addressed the Secretary of State, pointing out that the expediency of constructing an extension across the river at Barrakur had first been suggested some years previously, that the Directors were satisfied that it was desirable, but that hitherto they had been unable to obtain the assent of the Government of India; that further enquiry had confirmed their previous views, and had shewn the expediency of giving a somewhat greater extension to the line than at first contemplated.

The Board, not having been able to obtain consent to the original proposal, appear to have anticipated further delay in obtaining Government sanction to the larger scheme, and therefore adopted every means in their power to convince the Secretary of State of the desirability of constructing the extension without loss of time. In their letter they not only pointed out that there were good grounds for believing that the projected line would prove remunerative at an early period, but referred again to their general policy in regard to the coal traffic in the following terms :—

"As Lord Cross is aware, the Board have recently, with his Lordship's assent, made important reductions in the coal tariff, with a view to doing all that was within their power to develop and assist this important industry, and they think it is no more than reasonable to look forward, if proper facilities are provided, to the possible future development of a large export trade of coal from Calcutta, the commercial value of which, if successful, it would not be easy to exaggerate With this in view they will continue to do all in their power to extend and facilitate the economical working of the Bengal coal-fields, and they regard the present project as likely to be highly advantageous to the community generally."

After some delay the Secretary of State approved of the construction of the Jherriah extension; in 1892 the Government of India sanctioned the work, and it was at once started. On the 20th May 1894 trains began running as far as Ghootrya, some seven miles beyond Barrakur, the first train carrying 100 tons of coal and 50 passengers!

From such small beginnings do great things come when enterprise is guided by intelligent foresight. In less than three years the wisdom of the policy of the Railway Company was fully established, for by 1897 the collieries on the Jherriah and Toposi branch lines, the latter having been extended at the same time as the Jherriah branch, were contributing not far from a million tons a year to the traffic of the undertaking. It must not be thought that there was no real difficulty in obtaining sanction to the construction work proposed by the Company; on the contrary Government opinion for some time appeared opposed to expenditure, on what some of its responsible officers thought might prove an unprofitable undertaking. A certain Consulting Engineer to Government, whose opinions ordinarily carried great weight, held the view that the Jherriah branch would never pay, and that it was not wanted, but General Strachey persisted when others might have given way in despair. At a meeting of the shareholders in 1891, he publicly urged his case, saying :—

"It is a subject of continued regret and disappointment that the Government still withholds its decision as to the proposals of the Board for constructing the branch line from Barrakur to the Jherriah coal-field. The position of the Company under its contract with the Secretary of State, in respect to the provision of additional Capital, has unquestionably had a most unfortunate effect in crippling the Board in its attempts to carry out extensions of the undertaking, and the responsibility for any failure in this direction does not rest with them. It is not easy to understand how the Indian Government, which constantly professes its anxiety for the extension of railways, when it can be shown that they are likely to be profitable and can be undertaken without adding to the burdens on the State, is able to reconcile such professions with its passive resistance to the Board's proposals, or how it can appropriate the enormous profits made from the East Indian Railway, without an apparent thought of the claims of districts that have provided these large sums, to obtain extensions and amelioration of their means of communication, in carrying out which the Board is not only ready but most anxious to participate."

It must be remembered that in these days there was little or no public opinion to support General Strachey ; the Jherriah coal-field was known only to a few; the land was all in the hands of natives, who had no idea of its value, and in fact, but for the coal beneath it, it had no value. It was merely a bare uncultivated waste, the true value of which was quite unsuspected.

But as soon as the East Indian Railway constructed a line into the centre of the field, Coal Companies were formed, sidings applied for faster than they could be put in, and a rush of traffic came which was so sudden that it was almost beyond the power of the railway to carry it. The consequence was that the railway, while making the most strenuous efforts to provide additional facilities, was blamed instead of thanked, and the public, thinking no doubt that competition would lead to further reductions in rates, clamoured for the admission to the field of the Bengal-Nagpur Railway. The Government allowed this other line in, to compete for the traffic of the Jherriah collieries, created by the enterprise of the East Indian Railway alone. But after this was accomplished the Bengal-Nagpur Railway found that it could not compete for the important Calcutta traffic because of its longer lead to that port, and because of the fact that the Government would not allow it to quote rates for the traffic below the sanctioned minimum, such rates being necessary to equalize with the low charges made, before its entry, by the East Indian Railway. So far as the Government, the

Bengal-Nagpur Railway and the public were concerned, the entry of this line into the Jherriah coal-field was more or less a fiasco and matters were at a dead-lock, when the East Indian Railway Company, following its usual liberal policy, came to the rescue, and induced the Government to allow the Bengal-Nagpur Railway to quote equal rates with it, and so participate in a share of the Calcutta traffic, which undoubtedly belonged to them alone.

Such in brief is the history of the Jherriah coal-field, and a few figures of the traffic derived from it will suffice to prove its great importance.

* * * * *

COAL TRAFFIC FROM JHERRIAH BRANCH.

	Tons.
1894	38,831
1899	1,310,397
1905	2,827,725

CHAPTER XV.
COAL RATES.

IT will be remembered that in 1889 the Government of India claimed that coal, carried by the East Indian Railway Company, for the use of State Railways, should be charged at a uniform rate of 1-10th pie per maund per mile, and when General Strachey visited India this claim was very fully investigated by him. He examined the subject from a statistical point of view, and proved that there were very grave misconceptions as to the cost of carrying traffic by railway, and that the actual cost of transport, so far from being as low as $\frac{1}{10}$th pie per maund per mile was then really about half-way between $\frac{1}{4}$th and $\frac{1}{3}$th pie.

But while this was his estimate of the average cost of carriage of all classes of goods, General Strachey recognised that the transport of coal justified the demand for a lower rate than the average and proposed a scale, varying according to distance, of $\frac{1}{3}$rd to $\frac{1}{8}$th pie per maund per mile, with a rebate of 5 per cent on the total freight charges, whenever more than $1\frac{1}{2}$ lakh of maunds were carried in any half-year. General Strachey, in making this proposal, firmly deprecated the Goverment suggestion that State Railways should be charged a lower rate than others. To quote his own words : "there is no sufficient ground for treating railways worked by State Agency differently from those worked by Companies."

Such was the position in the beginning of 1890, and it did not take long for the Government to recognise the soundness of the arguments put forward. The claim to the $\frac{1}{10}$th pie rate was given up, and it was admitted that all railways, whether State or otherwise, should be treated alike. But during the discussion further developments arose, and the outcome was that the whole question of the coal tariff was placed before General Strachey, as Chairman of the East Indian Railway, and General Williams, then Deputy Government Director for Indian Guaranteed Railways.

These two jointly drew up a scale of charges, and recommended that they should apply to all customers alike, whether railway administrations in the hands of the Government, or Companies, manufacturing firms or exporters or other traders, and the Secretary of State, having accepted them, requested the Goverment of India to take the necessary steps to put them in force as early as possible.

Briefly stated the proposed tariff was as follows :—

    (a) For all stations up to 400 miles 0·15 pie per maund per mile.

(b) For all stations over 400 miles, for the first 400 miles according to clause (a), for distances in excess 0·10 pie per maund per mile.

These rates were subject to a scale of rebates for large consignments, and certain rules were detailed as to routing and so forth. In accepting them the Board of Directors of the East Indian Railway wrote to the Secretary of State, on the 4th August 1891, in the following terms:—

"The Board readily assent to the proposals in question and trust that the important concessions to the public in respect of the coal tariff, which they embody, will be productive of much general advantage.

"The Board are fully impressed with the great importance to all Indian interests of increasing the facilities for the supply of cheap coal, and they look forward with much hopefulness to the early establishment of an export traffic of coal from Calcutta, the value of which it would be almost impossible to exaggerate, not only as regards the coal owners, but to all Indian industries, and they trust that their endeavours to realize such a result may receive the support of the Secretary of State and the Government of India.

"It will be the desire of the Board to carry out to the fullest extent, that experience may shew to be reasonable and practicable, the reduction in the charges for the transport of coal over the undertaking, and they quite recognise that the tariff, which it is now proposed to adopt, will be subject to reconsideration should this hereafter be found desirable."

Thus was this all important subject settled, not in India but in London, not on the narrow lines suggested by the Government of India, but on the broad principle that there should be no differential treatment of the customers of a railway, or, in other words, that a rate given to one should equally apply to all. The general effect of the new arrangement was to give a substantial reduction in the rates for all distances, amounting to about 15 per cent, and this required a corresponding increase of traffic to maintain the revenue at its former level, but at the time no uneasiness was felt, for, as the Chairman remarked, "the growth of the coal traffic leaves no room fo doubting the early realization of the requisite increase and gives reasonable ground for expecting still further and more satisfactory expansion in the future."

That the expectations of the Home Board in respect to the growth of the coal traffic were fully realized is proved in a few words. In 1891 the freight earnings of the East Indian Railway from coal were little more than 63 lakhs of rupees, in the year 1896 they had risen to over 97 lakhs, and in 1901 to over 180 lakhs. This enormous expansion of traffic will be dealt with more fully in another chapter, suffice to say here that the scale of charges, drawn up by Generals Strachey and Williams in ~~1901~~ [1891] remained in force without material alteration for many years and was accepted, not only by the East Indian, but generally speaking by all the railways in India.

Naturally, as time went on and experience was gained of the practical working of the new coal rates, certain modifications were found desirable, but these, whether in the rules or in the rates, were all in the nature of concessions to the trade, notably an additional rebate of 10 per cent on coal exported by sea, together with certain other changes of rule introduced in 1895; but in the main the 1891 scale remained in force until 1902 and during this period the traffic developed more rapidly than the facilities required to deal with it could be introduced. As early as 1893 there was under serious consideration a proposal to construct a short branch line, from Bally Station to a point on the river just below the Botanical Gardens, where it was thought that a coal jetty equipped with mechanical loading appliances would greatly facilitate the export trade, but like the Luff Point Scheme, which followed many years later, the idea was abandoned, after it had got as far as being recommended to the Government. Proposals of this nature and proposals actually carried out, with the object of improving facilities for dealing with the general expansion of traffic, and particularly of the coal trade, hardly come within the province of this chapter, and we may pass on to the next great change in the coal tariff inaugurated by General Sir Richard Strachey in 1902. It must not, however, be supposed that this last change was suddenly adopted, as some have thought, as a protective measure, because of the entry of the Bengal-Nagpur Railway into the Jherriah field; on the contrary, it had been contemplated for many years before that time, but various considerations necessitated delay; among these we need only mention the shortness of wagon stock, congestion of traffic on the running lines and inadequate shipping facilities. During the whole period in which the 1891 tariff was in force the growth of the coal traffic was most closely watched, and, as early as 1896, further concessions were mooted, though it had not then been established that any grounds existed for reductions; on the contrary, the continued expansion of the trade during the previous five years supported an opposite view. Various aspects of the question were discussed from time to time, but, although minor concessions were granted, as for instance the reduction in the weight required to be put into wagons in order to obtain the "full wagon" rates, any substantial modification of the tariff had to be deferred. As a matter of fact, in 1898, the Board proposed, to their Agent in India, certain material reductions in charges from the Jherriah and Toposi branches, in order to place the collieries in those fields in a better position than they were, compared with fields nearer Calcutta, but these also were deferred because there was a rise in the price of coal, and the Jherriah field, as evidenced by the traffic carried, was in no way hampered by the charges in force. Beyond this, Colonel Gardiner, the then Agent of the Company, feared that to give a large reduction to the Jherriah coal-field, except as a part of a complete scheme, would raise an outcry from collieries lower down the line.

In June 1902, however, the Board of Directors revealed a complete scheme of revision, and in doing so pointed out that they had had the question before them since 1898, remarking that "until now circumstances have not admitted of action being taken in the direction contemplated." The tariff introduced in 1891 was reviewed, and it was shewn that, with the modifications from time to time introduced, it had been consistent with a great development of the trade. The rebate system was commented upon, and the opinion expressed that, so far as the ordinary coal traffic was concerned, it was not necessary or convenient and should not be perpetuated. Its abolition would benefit small consignors. But, for a variety of reasons, the special treatment of export coal was held to be established and a special rebate on such coal would therefore be continued.

The Board's proposal was to introduce the following tariff for coal in full wagon loads:—

For distances up to 75 miles inclusive ... 0·14 pie per maund per mile.
Plus for any distance in excess of 75 miles and up to 200 miles inclusive ... 0·12 ,, ,, ,,
Plus for any distance in excess of 200 miles and up to 450 miles inclusive ... 0·10 ,, ,, ,,
Plus for any distance in excess of 450 miles and up to 1,000 miles inclusive ... 0·09 ,, ,, ,,

A rebate of 20 per cent to be allowed on all coal exported, no other rebates being allowed.

These proposals were at once adopted, although it was estimated that the reductions involved a sacrifice of about 20 lakhs of rupees per annum. The benefit to the trade was as fairly distributed as possible to all consumers; great encouragement was given to long lead traffic and to the export trade, while in no case did the withdrawal of rebate on inland traffic cause hardship. On the contrary each consignor got the equivalent or more at the time of despatch, instead of several months afterwards, and the inconvenience of calculating rebate dues was at once put an end to.

The nicety of the calculations involved in introducing this revision of the coal tariff, its completeness and general suitability were entirely due to General Sir Richard Strachey, by whose hand the scheme was drawn up, and it seems evident from the trial already given to it that this tariff has proved an undoubted success.

In his address to the shareholders on the traffic of the first half of 1903, Sir Richard Strachey referred to this matter in the following terms :—

"I may be excused for taking this opportunity for formally repudiating the suggestion, recently made by the Agent of the Bengal-Nagpur Railway Company, that the introduction of the new coal tariff on the East Indian Railway last year was designed to prejudice the development of the coal traffic of the Bengal-Nagpur line. The suggestion appears to me to be so absurd on the face of it as hardly to have called for notice, but the boldness of attributing to the Board of this Company, the deliberate intention of sacrificing, for such an object, receipts amounting to some 20 lakhs of rupees in the year, is such, that persons having no knowledge of the facts might not unreasonably suppose that the suggestion could not have been made, unless it were based on some ground of fact. I therefore have thought it right to refer to the matter. The revised tariff, which was adopted with the objects I have mentioned, had the approval of the Government of India. The correspondence has been recently published in India, and will show that there was no sort of foundation for the imputation to which I have referred, which was put forward as evidence in relation to the project for establishing an export coaling station on the Hooghly, below Calcutta, with the merits of which, the motives that led to the reduced charges for transport on the East Indian Railway, could have no possible connection "

Recently a further scheme of reduced rates for coal has come under consideration, but it is hoped that before it is generally introduced the question of wagon stock, in which to carry any large accession of traffic, will not be lost sight of. If the rates are reduced before the railways are ready with a considerable increase to their facilities, there will be no benefit to the trade but rather the reverse. At the present time more wagons are in coal than in all the rest of the traffic of the East Indian Railway put together, that is to say, more wagons are loaded every day in the colliery district alone, than in all the other districts of the line taken together, and yet the railway is short of requirements.

CHAPTER XVI.

GROWTH OF THE COAL TRAFFIC.

NOTHING in the history of the East Indian Railway has been more remarkable than the growth of the coal traffic during the past 15 years. Up to the year 1889 few had recognised its immense possibilities, and there was certainly no idea of a great export trade setting in, while internal requirements were comparatively small and restricted almost entirely to the needs of railways. There seems to have been at the outset a good deal of prejudice on the part of those who had previously burnt Welsh coal, and particularly on the part of the engineers of the larger steamship companies, against the introduction of Bengal coal in its place; these prejudices were only overcome by degrees, but once a start had been made the import of coal from the United Kingdom was doomed. In the first half of the year 1885, more than 45,000 tons of Welsh coal were imported into Calcutta, during the first half of 1889 the quantity imported dropped to less than 1,000 tons, and an export trade then started, principally in bunker coal for the use of the steamers of the British India Steam Navigation Company, which extended even more rapidly than the most sanguine anticipated. In 1890 the growth of the export of Bengal coal from Calcutta first attracted serious attention, though in proportion to the total downwards traffic the export figures were still comparatively small. Rangoon was the port which at first took the largest quantity; Bombay, which is now the largest taker of Bengal coal, adhering very largely to the Welsh product until some years afterwards.

In 1891 the want of facilities for dealing with a large coal traffic were recognised. The Traffic Manager, Mr. J. Rutherford, commenting on the expansion which would follow the opening up of numerous mines in the coalfields adjacent to Asansol and Sitarampur and of the Jherriah field, an extension to which was then about to be started, remarked that "we have neither the wagon stock nor the terminal accommodation required for such an accession to our traffic," and strongly advocated the construction by the Railway Company of special jetties and loading machinery at a point on the river below the Botanical Gardens, to which he proposed a short branch line should be run from Bally Station, a few miles above the Howrah terminus. The upwards coal traffic was also growing, the different railways in the North-West, Oudh and Punjab were consuming more, though the use of coal for domestic purposes was nominal, and in places like Cawnpore, which was rapidly becoming the internal centre of commercial enterprise, wood was still burnt extensively in preference.

In the year 1893 the export trade from Calcutta had grown to about 250,000 tons, and towards the close of the year, the Kidderpore Docks, constructed for the receipt of ordinary merchandise, were first brought into use for loading export cargoes of coal. It was, however, anticipated that the docks would not at all meet the requirements of the trade, and that if the rapidly growing business was to be dealt with there, considerable additions would be needed, while the railway approaches would also have to be improved. The opening of the docks to export coal traffic at once brought the Jubilee Bridge over the Hooghly into use; previous to this time it had been more or less a white elephant, for very little business of any kind had been done at the docks. In the second half of 1892 about 189,000 tons of all classes of traffic were carried over the bridge, in the second half of 1893 the weight rose to 345,000 tons, of which two-thirds were coal. In 1894 there was a still further advance in the export coal trade, and General Sir Richard Strachey forecast, in an address to the shareholders of the Company, what the future was likely to be: "There is no possible reason," he remarked, "why the whole of the coal now exported from England, whether required on land, or for consumption at sea east of Aden, should not be replaced by Indian coal."

By 1895 the Toposi and Jherriah colliery branches were partially opened and immediately there followed a great accession of traffic, new mines were opened out in all directions and it became a difficulty for the engineers to keep pace with the demands for sidings to the different collieries. From this time onward the coal traffic increased by leaps and bounds, and it was in the export trade that the increase was most noticeable; in 1891 the export trade of Calcutta amounted to 137,000 tons, in 1896 it had risen to 574,000 tons, in 1901 to 1,995,000 tons, and in 1905 to 2,767,000 tons. It would be tedious to attempt to traverse the great difficulties in working a traffic which had expanded so suddenly; the shortness of stock, the inadequate terminal facilities, the congestion on the line owing to the want of engine power and of proper marshalling yards and so forth had all to be overcome, and nothing could be done sufficiently quickly to materially ease the position. Many schemes were put forward, many proposals discussed, and throughout the time of greatest trial, the Home Board not only gave strong support to the efforts of the staff in India, but continuously pressed on the Government the crying need for more wagons, more sidings, better facilities and so forth, but relief was only too tardily granted in some cases and declined altogether in others. Addressing the shareholders in June 1897, General Sir Richard Strachey said :—

> "There can be little doubt that the Bengal coal trade has a great future before it, and that its increasing requirements will demand constant attention and a further considerable development of the means of transport and facilities for shipping for export. I cannot think that the export of coal on a large scale, and I would remind you that it has already risen to more than half a million of tons in the half-year, can be conveniently or economically carried on from docks designed to meet the requirements of the ordinary export and import trade of a commercial centre like Calcutta. It is therefore in my opinion a matter of regret that a more comprehensive view of this question has not been taken and that arrangements have not been made, as was proposed by the Board some years ago, for establishing a system of coal export, more closely following what experience, on a very large scale in this country, has shown to be best suited for this special class of business. The wisdom of the policy of extending the coal lines in Bengal, to which the Board have been able to give effect by constructing the Jherriah and Toposi branches, is now fully established, and the new collieries on them are already contributing not far from a million tons a year to the traffic of the undertaking."

In subsequent addresses General Sir Richard Strachey referred, over and over again, to the pressing needs for better facilities and for more rolling stock, and over and over again defended the management of the railway against the not infrequent attacks of the mercantile community, whose complaints of want of wagons, or of blocks of traffic, resulting, as they alleged, in loss of business, were at the time common. At a meeting of the shareholders held in December 1901, the

Chairman spoke very plainly, and his words, which proved most prophetic, are worth quoting. He said :—

"As the coal owners of Bengal are among the most persistent of those who exclaim against the management of the East Indian Railway, and of the want of attention paid to their interests, I will venture to call their attention to the following statement of the present value of the coal properties in Bengal, properties that, as I have already said, have been entirely created by the initiative of the railway, and the continued prosperity of which has been ensured by equally constant attention to their requirements. The extremely low rates at which coal has been carried on all Indian railways for the last ten years is also due to the action of the East Indian Railway ; the opening out of the Jherriah coalfield, which was opposed by the Government of India, was at last sanctioned by an appeal to the Secretary of State by the Board."

Present value of shares in Bengal Coal Companies—

	Paid up	Quotation.
	Rs.	Rs.
Adjai	100	250-255
Bengal	1,000	3,150
Bengal-Nagpur	10	30¾
Borrea	100	155
Barrakur	100	125
Equitable	100	262
Katras-Jherriah	10	40½
New Beerbhoom	100	179
Reliance	100	190

"I have no wish," he added, "to be a prophet of evil, but there is an opinion afloat, which seems deserving of serious attention, that the very rapid development of the coal trade, accompanied, as it has been, by this remarkable inflation of values, may be the forerunner of a season of speculative mining enterprise, and of over production, in excess of the growing requirements of the public."

Within a year of the time these words were spoken their truth became apparent, the output of the collieries became much larger than a market could be found for and share quotations declined with a run. Fortunately the check was only a temporary one, and lost ground was soon regained.

Nothing, however, will better illustrate the rapid growth of the coal traffic than the following brief statement, shewing the weight carried and the earnings during periods separated by five years:—

Year.	Total coal traffic.	Up.	Down.	Exported.	Total earnings.
	Tons.	Tons.	Tons.	Tons.	Rs.
1889	1,404,711	303,910	1,100,801	not available.	64,26,925
1894	2,144,382	466,768	1,677,614	297,000	79,51,472
1899	3,897,596	630,544	3,267,052	1,136,000	135,29,685
1905	6,142,264	1,260,740	4,881,524	2,767,000	202,44,250

These figures speak for themselves, and call for no comment beyond the remark that they are an eloquent testimony to the part played by the East Indian Railway Company. In the early days of development allusion was often made to the undertaking having what was termed a monopoly of the transport, and it was clearly intimated that such a monopoly was prejudicial to development. The Board of Directors naturally took exception to such views, unsupported as they were by facts, and in 1894 expressed their opinion very clearly in the following words:—

"A monopoly that is used to keep up prices to the detriment of trade cannot be too strongly deprecated, but such a necessary monopoly as that enjoyed by the East Indian

Railway, in respect of the traffic over its own line, conducted on the principle of reducing the rates to a minimum and of working in the most economical manner, is a positive advantage to the public, and to destroy it by introducing any intermediate agency, which could only lead to additional unnecessary expenditure would be an act of folly. The conditions under which the traffic of the East Indian Railway is conducted render excessive charges impossible, and the well-known facts of the case clearly shew that the Board have made very important reductions of charge, which may reasonably be taken to indicate that their policy is a liberal one and that they intend to persevere in it so far as they are able."

"The Board have seen with much satisfaction that the downward coal traffic has responded in a very marked manner to the reductions already made in the tariff. It is their firm conviction that, by judicious arrangements, the traffic may be brought into a condition that will admit of further important reductions of charge, and, unless obstacles are put in their way, they look forward to practical effect being given to this anticipation."

The point of these remarks seems to be that, whatever detractors may say, there is no getting over the fact that the interests of the Railway Company and of the trade are identical; and that the Railway Company has done all in its power to foster and develop the coal traffic of Bengal is clearly proved by results. During the past six years the raisings of Bengal coal have increased from four to seven million tons annually and the trade generally has never been so prosperous as at the present time. But it is not only by reducing rates, and by opening up the coalfields adjacent to its main line, in the Asansol and Barrakur Districts, that the East Indian Railway Company has assisted in developing the great traffic it now carries. There was still another field within its territory, namely the Daltonganj field in the Sasseram District, 150 miles nearer the north-west than the coalfields of Bengal proper. This field was also opened up by the East Indian Railway Company and now forms an additional source of supply. Although it has not, so far, proved of any great value, still its opening goes to prove that the Company has at heart the interests of the public.

For some years the coal traffic has been of such importance to the East Indian Railway that an annual report on its principal features is submitted to the Home Board. It need only be added that in every direction efforts are made to comply, as fully as possible, with the wishes of the coal owners for modifications of the traffic arrangements that they regard as likely to be beneficial, but difficulties in the way can only be overcome by degrees, however willing the management may be to carry them through.

CHAPTER XVII.

THE KIDDERPORE DOCKS.

AT the time that General Strachey was appointed Chairman of the East Indian Railway Company, the Kidderpore Docks were being constructed and there was much discussion as to the rates that would be charged on traffic booked to and from the new terminus.

The Jubilee Bridge across the Hooghly River had been opened for traffic a short time before, and trains were running over it as far as the Chitpore and Sealdah termini of the Eastern Bengal Railway in Calcutta, a provisional arrangement having been come to, under which traffic carried to these stations should be charged the same as if carried to the East Indian Railway terminus of Howrah and vice versa.

It was agreed that no compulsion should be used to force ships into the docks, and therefore all facilities at Howrah, which in the course of years had become the established centre for the receipt and despatch of merchandise, had to be preserved intact. Beyond this the East Indian Railway was saddled with the interest on the cost of the Jubilee Bridge, for which until then it had received practically no compensation, while extensive alterations and additions had become necessary at Hooghly Junction, in order to enable the railway to make up full train loads for the termini on the Calcutta side of the river. Therefore the question of the rates to be charged on traffic hauled by East Indian Railway trains to the Kidderpore Docks was an important one.

The Government of India held the opinion that "there should not be any difference in freight charges on up-country through goods consigned to or from Calcutta, whether they are dealt with at Howrah or at Kidderpore", but the Eastern Bengal Railway Company, over which the trains had to be hauled to the docks, claimed a rate of two rupees per train mile on every East Indian Railway train passing Naihati Junction, and the Board could not see their way to paying so excessive a rate and at the same time making no additional charge to the public.

The Board, however, wished to do all in their power to assist the trade of the port, and therefore proposed to the Government that if for East Indian Railway trains running to Sealdah, Chitpore or the Kidderpore Docks the Eastern Bengal Railway Company would accept one rupee per train mile on the actual distance run, they on their part would be prepared to charge the public the same rate to any of these places as to Howrah.

Finally, a compromise was arrived at, the Eastern Bengal Railway Company agreed to reduce the train mile rate of two rupees on trains run to Chitpore and Sealdah to one rupee eight annas, and to accept a rate of twelve annas per train mile on trains run to the docks, charges to the public being the same in all cases as the charge on traffic for Howrah, and this arrangement, being agreed to by the East Indian Railway, has remained in force to the present day.

So much for the question of rates. The docks had been constructed mainly for the grain and seed traffic; there was no idea of coal being dealt with there; no idea, in fact, that an export coal trade would ever set in; but almost from the day of opening the coal trade forced itself upon the docks. Coal has now become the principal traffic consigned there. Coal berths have been constructed and added to, but still the accommodation is barely sufficient for the requirements of the trade and more additions are contemplated. It is only in recent seasons, however, that the grain and seed traffic has gone to the docks; for many years the sheds constructed to deal with this traffic lay empty and idle, the merchants preferring to work at Howrah, where their business had so long been established. In 1898, or several years after the docks had been opened for traffic, General Strachey addressing the shareholders said :—" No perceptible effect has yet been produced on the trade arrangements of Calcutta by the partial opening of the docks, to which very few vessels have hitherto resorted. Difficulties have arisen, that had not been foreseen, in inducing traders to modify the practice that has hitherto prevailed, as to loading and unloading ships, when lying at their moorings in the river, by means of lighters, and these have not yet been so far overcome as to bring about any general movement of the export trade to the docks, to meet which all requisite preliminary arrangements have been made. It is, however, hardly likely that an alteration of system can be very long delayed."

It was in 1898 that, in consequence of a block of wheat at Howrah, the traffic was for a few days diverted to the docks, only to block the shed accommodation there also; and in 1899 the docks actually declined to receive grain and seeds except under restrictions, as the authorities feared a repetition of their experience of the previous year, a fear that was shared by the merchants who had suffered from the resulting confusion.

The aversion on the part of the trade to utilising the accommodation at the docks was in no way due to the action of the East Indian Railway; on the contrary the East Indian Railway had done all in its power to promote the use of the sheds available there; but the mercantile community did little to overcome difficulties, although it was a matter of vital interest to them, for the trade of the port was burdened to provide means for paying the interest on the capital outlay and the cost of maintaining the docks, from which no advantage was being obtained. "It is certainly difficult," the Chairman had said in 1893, "for any one like myself, not acquainted in detail with the circumstances of the case, not to feel surprise that the mercantile community, which would seem to be so greatly interested in this matter, should treat it with such apparent indifference." General Strachey repeatedly advocated measures to assist the trade of Calcutta, by transferring the bulk of the export and import work to the docks, but it was years before the change was accomplished, and then more by the force of circumstances than by the action of those most interested. And in the meantime, year after year, as regularly as the season came round for exporting grain and seeds, the Howrah terminus became blocked and the East Indian Railway congested with traffic. For this the East Indian Railway management was invariably blamed, though it was repeatedly explained that the blocks of traffic were actually due to no fault on the part of the railway, but were caused by the consignees of goods being *unable* or unwilling to take delivery at Howrah, on the arrival of the wagons carrying the goods. In 1899 General Sir Richard Strachey remarked that "notwithstanding the efforts made to attract the export trade from Howrah to the docks the bulk of it is still dealt with at Howrah, partly because the dock charges are in many cases in excess of those incurred by shipping with boats from Howrah, but mainly owing to a large number of the up-country traders finding the Howrah terminus to be more convenient, as it offers facilities for certain classes of export produce changing hands, which the conditions of the trade require."

In 1901 a change came over the scene, only a small portion of the export produce passing through the docks, the Howrah terminus became, as usual, as full as it could be, and some measure of relief had to be decided upon. The Wheat and Seeds Association and the principal export firms were consulted, and with their assent it was decided to temporarily close Howrah to the receipt of linseed. The experiment proved successful, the linseed went to the docks, and ever since then the docks have been the chief centre for the export of linseed, while a considerable proportion of the wheat trade is also dealt with there.

During the year 1897 the total traffic crossing the Jubilee Bridge amounted to 2,040,686 tons; in 1901 the figures rose to

3,613,451, the proportions of coal and ordinary merchandise being :—

	Coal.	Ordinary merchandise.
1897	1,582,557	458,129
1901	2,995,600	617,851

At the present time over $4\frac{1}{2}$ million tons of traffic cross the Jubilee Bridge yearly, of which more than two million tons consist of coal exported from the Kidderpore Docks, where there are eight coal-loading berths, one of which is provided with a mechanical loading appliance. An increase of three more coaling berths is now contemplated, and, judging by the continued growth of the trade, they will not be provided at all too soon. In other ways also the accommodation at the Kidderpore Docks has in recent years been vastly improved; generally speaking the docks are now on a level with trade requirements.

CHAPTER XVIII.

TRAIN SERVICE AND WORKING FACILITIES—
THE QUESTION OF WAGON SUPPLY.

WHEN General Strachey visited India in 1889 he found that the train service was exceedingly slow. What was described as the "fast train" took no less than $37\frac{1}{2}$ hours to cover the distance of 954 miles between Howrah and Delhi, that is to say, it trundled along at a through speed of little more than 25 miles an hour; while consignments of goods occupied weeks in transit where they should have taken days.

Everything in the way of progress seemed to have been neglected, nothing was up-to-date. The stations were not interlocked; the out-door signals and the train signalling apparatus were of the most primitive kind; passenger carriages were illuminated with vegetable oil lamps, which only served to make darkness visible, and not a single engine or vehicle was fitted with a vacuum brake. In addition to this, the conditions of working were risky, if not dangerous, for over the greater portion of the line "following trains" were allowed, and it was only over a comparatively short section of double line that the "absolute block" system was in force.

With such a state of affairs there was obviously a crying need for remedy.

General Strachey during his stay in India wrote a note on the speed of the mail trains, in which he drew attention to the excessive number of stoppages *en route*, and suggested a revised time-table. This time-table was shortly afterwards adopted and reduced the run of the mail between Howrah and Delhi from $37\frac{1}{2}$ to $31\frac{1}{2}$ hours. At the same time he insisted upon an immediate revision of the goods train service, with the result that, early in 1890, a fast through goods train was run from Howrah to Cawnpore, and a very great saving effected in the time of transit of through booked goods; but even these improvements were not sufficient, and as soon as the Chairman returned to England, the Board wrote suggesting further accelerations. Ever since then the Chairman has continued to devote personal attention towards effecting improvements; he has closely watched the running of trains, commenting each half-year on the time actually taken over the different sections of the line, so that the staff know well that punctuality of the train service is considered all important; in addition to this there has been no measure towards improvement that has not had his cordial support.

At the present time the absolute block system is in force throughout the entire length of the line; all coaching vehicles are fitted with vacuum automatic brakes; goods vehicles are being so fitted and their carrying capacity has been materially increased; the majority of stations are either interlocked or are being interlocked; the signalling has been greatly improved and the train service has been very much accelerated. The mail train, with a load equal to eighteen heavy coaches, now runs from Howrah to Delhi in $28\frac{1}{2}$ hours, and lighter trains have been run over the same distance in very little more than 24 hours. Such speeds would have been impossible even five years ago, for it took a long time to carry out the many improvements required, to enable the staff in India to work up to such results.

In the meantime the difficulties to be contended with, whenever traffic was at all brisk, were enormous. Year after year the line below Asansol became blocked with trains, that could not be got through because the terminals were glutted with goods, and because there was an utter absence of proper facilities for dealing with the traffic that had grown with such rapidity. Progress seemed slow, but by the year 1902, such improvements had been effected that an exceptionally heavy traffic was carried, for the first time, without congestion. The General Traffic Manager in his report on the results of the working during the first half of that year remarked—

"Perhaps the most satisfactory feature of the half-year's traffic was that even when at its highest, we were able to

IMPROVED TRAIN LOADS.

put it through without any block at Howrah or on the line, and without a single complaint of short wagon supplies. This was due to a combination of causes, notably the increase in upwards coal traffic, giving our wagons going up country for grain, a load in both directions and so minimising delay for stock; the linseed traffic being dealt with at Kidderpore Docks, from the start, instead of only being dealt with there when Howrah got into difficulties; a comparatively small wheat traffic; an improved supply of brake-vans and engines, together with other favourable influences, unnecessary to detail, which rendered the movement of the traffic easier than it has been for several years."

These remarks almost read in the nature of an apology for the season's work being accomplished without any of the difficulties that had beset the staff in previous years, but the fact is that, facilities had improved, and their effect was for the first time showing itself; even under the most favourable circumstances the traffic could not have been properly dealt with unless this had been so. Since 1902 the line has never been blocked, although a still heavier traffic has been carried, and carried with greater expedition than was possible under the old method of working. This result has not, however, been altogether due to the better facilities provided but to the increased attention given to the improvement of train and wagon loads. During the past few years the average load of a goods train has been greatly increased. In the first half of 1902 it was 202·75 tons; in the first half of 1903, 226·97 tons; in the second half of 1903, it rose to 243 tons; in the first half of 1904 to 252·58 tons; and in the second half of the same year to 276 tons.

An increased train load meant fewer, but heavier trains, fewer engines, fewer brake-vans and a considerable saving in coal and staff; this question is only mentioned here as one of the causes that have facilitated the passing of a heavy traffic over the line, though this perhaps is the least important sequence of a measure that has resulted in most important economies.

Speaking to the shareholders in 1903, General Sir Richard Strachey referred to the improved conditions of working in these terms :—

> "There is every reason to think that the improvements of various descriptions in the system of signalling and in providing for the more expeditious movement of the traffic, which have been in steady progress for some years past, have proved their value by increased freedom from obstructions, and facility in dealing with the traffic on the busiest parts of the line. Increased attention is being given to the great importance of improving the train loads, by which it is anticipated that large reductions in the train mileage may be secured and corresponding economies, both in the cost of running and of the rolling stock required for the traffic moved."

A word may here be said on the question of wagon stock. Following the rapid development of traffic and particularly of the coal traffic which has been the most marked feature, in recent years, of the Company's administration, there have been constant difficulties in regard to the supply of locomotives, wagons and brake-vans. Within the past few years the locomotive and brake-van difficulty has been overcome, the line is no longer congested, whenever traffic is brisk, and engine or brake-van shortage is hardly, if ever, heard of; but still the wagon supply continues inadequate. At the present time very bitter complaints are being made, more especially by those interested in the coal trade, that stock requirements are not met in the way they should be.

In the year 1900 the wagon stock of the East Indian Railway was under 14,000 wagons, in 1905 it was over 17,000 wagons; in other words, the wagon stock has been increased by about 24 per cent in five years. The weight of goods traffic, including coal, has increased during the same period by 21 per cent, yet during some period or another there has been shortage of stock.

There is, certainly, a reverse side to the picture; whenever traffic at all slackens hundreds of wagons lie idle in sidings, and it is a fact that the traffic of the East Indian Railway fluctuates very greatly. It is doubtful whether the railway could possibly provide a stock equal to all demands at periods of highest pressure; it is doubtful whether any railway in the world of like size has ever been able to do so. Certainly shortness of stock due to rushes of traffic, or to congestion of the line, or to block at the terminals or elsewhere, is not peculiar to the East Indian Railway. We have heard of the same sort of thing happening in America on some of the best equipped lines, and so long as railways exist, and have to be worked at a profit, as indeed all commercial enterprises must be, shortness of stock will occasionally be felt.

Could the traffic of the East Indian Railway be evenly distributed over every week of the year, we should never hear of shortness of stock, but this is clearly impossible, and admitting that there is even occasional shortage, the question arises, what surplus should be provided in order to meet requirements when traffic is above normal, for obviously there should be some surplus. As a general basis of regulating supply, it has been calculated that every wagon should carry 75,000 ton miles of traffic in half a year; this means a very full use of the available stock. Still it has been worked to, and sometimes exceeded in the past, and is, perhaps, a sufficiently liberal allowance for the future. There are times, however, when an excessive number of East Indian Railway wagons have to be sent away with loads to Foreign Railways, and when Foreign Railway wagons are not coming to any great extent on to the East Indian; at these times the margin of work required becomes too tight. There are other times when the nature of the traffic is such that the best advantage cannot be obtained from the stock employed; then also there is shortage. Moreover, it may be admitted that a railway should be, within limits, ahead of requirements rather than behind them, but up to the present, except when working conditions have been most favourable, it has been difficult to keep pace with the development and expansion of traffic. When we find shortage continuing, month after month, for long periods at a stretch, there is little doubt that the railway is short of requirements. This is the present position, and although additions are now being made to the stock, which should minimise difficulties, it is not likely that complaints of shortage will altogether cease. If the additions sanctioned were ready and on the line at the present moment there would not be one too many wagons. It is hoped that, in anticipation of continued growth of the traffic, regular additions to the wagon stock will continue to be sanctioned every year, until the railway finds itself ahead of requirements.

CHAPTER XIX.

SOME FURTHER REMARKS on COMPETITION AND RATES.

ALTHOUGH the low charges at present in force on the East Indian Railway are mainly due to the liberal policy followed in voluntarily reducing the rates for such items as coal, still it must not be forgotten that a famine in Bengal first directed attention to the possibility of carrying traffic, over long distances, at charges which were previously considered impossible, and that competition has also had its effect on the tariff.

It has been shown that serious competition against the East Indian Railway began, when the opening of the Rajputana route to Bombay first threatened Calcutta with the diversion of the trade of the Upper Provinces. But the East Indian Railway has not had to contend with the rivalry of the Western lines alone; it has also had to meet the competition of various alternative railway routes and of rivers, canals and roads. To talk therefore of the East Indian Railway having a monopoly of traffic shows a strange misconception of facts.

Before the East Indian Railway has run 150 miles of its course from Calcutta it gets in touch with the River Ganges, the main waterway of Bengal, on which a service of competing steamers is ever ready to convey traffic to and from the metropolis, at rates far below those which would be profitable to the railway. That the railway is able to compete with these steamers is mainly due to the speedier transit it can offer and to the fact that during the monsoons, when steamers are best able to ply, the Railway is generally experiencing a slack time and is in a position to make special concessions in rates. These rates, known as "monsoon rates," are successful in drawing to the rail a share of the trade which it would otherwise lose, but in any case the direct effect is reduction.

As to native boats, these attempt to carry all they can from any source, but while they take something away they also bring something to the rail, and therefore may be regarded as feeders as well as competitors. It was in order to enable country boats to bring produce to the rail direct that branch lines were originally constructed to all the more important ghâts on the river bank; and, on the whole, although the river has been the cause of many rate reductions, it is really one of the best friends of the railway. The riparian stations on the East Indian Railway are among its most important.

Before the railway gets beyond the effect of river competition it has to contend with the claims of the Western lines which are always trying to draw to Bombay the traffic whose natural port is Calcutta. This competition begins within 500 miles of Calcutta and extends over the whole length of the railway above, including of course the Jubbulpore line, where, perhaps, the East.Indian Railway position is weakest.

The influence of competition is also felt with the Bengal-Nagpur Railway running by an alternative route to Kutni Station on the Jubbulpore branch ; with the Oudh and Rohilkhand Railway and connected systems running almost parallel, and tapping the East Indian at several points ; with the Bengal and North-Western which has gradually but surely extended its system on the other side of the River Ganges, and affects rates as high up as Delhi and even beyond ; with the Southern Punjab and North-Western Railways which endeavour to draw traffic to Kurrachee; not to mention railways which have been permitted to construct alternative routes, within the sphere of East Indian Railway control, such as the Agra-Delhi Chord and that greatest of all blunders, the Cawnpore-Achneyra line. It would form a history in itself to trace the effect of all the competition the East Indian Railway has to meet, to discuss the several agreements come to with foreign lines and to disentangle the many disagreements ; and even if this was done it would not be of great interest to any but traffic experts; it would not assist materially in judging the main results, which have been an exceedingly low, if complicated, tariff and an ever-increasing traffic.

The East Indian Railway has never feared fair competition, but there is a strong feeling that some restriction should be placed on lines which needlessly reduce charges at competitive points, and then, in order, apparently, to make up for the loss, retain their internal rates at an excessively high figure. The system of laying down a hard and fast rule for all railways, irrespective of the length of lead or of cost of working, in no way meets the case, especially when the absurdities of the methods resorted to on some systems are seen; but these have become more apparent since competition has grown keener, and the public are now beginning to appreciate the facts and to place them before the Government.

Speaking to the shareholders in 1891, General Sir Richard Strachey remarked :—
"The East Indian Railway has no cause to look with anxiety or jealousy at any increase of railway facilities offered by other lines, the traffic of the undertaking rests on a thoroughly sound, independent basis, and only needs a judicious system of management and a liberal tariff, such as the Board desires to offer to the public, to ensure its continued expansion."
General Sir Richard Strachey also accepts the view, which is undoubtedly correct, that

"if there is some loss by the diversion of traffic from the East Indian Railway that, in the absence of other lines, it might have retained, it is beyond question that any such result is largely compensated, if not actually counterbalanced, by the increased traffic due to the opening up of communication with districts formerly inaccessible." At the same time, the Board, while recognising that the traffic which is directed from the North-West Provinces towards Bombay, should be provided with whatever facilities it may require, fail to see why the East Indian Railway should be left powerless to respond to reductions because they are bound by a common minimum, although they can afford to carry at cheaper rates than any other line in India. If, as the Secretary of State says, " the advantages due either to geographical position or other circumstances " should furnish no reason for artificial restrictions, then what can be said of the restriction of a minimum rate, when a railway can carry at a profit below that minimum?

Then again, although the Board declined to recognise the claim of the railways, designed to carry the traffic of Central and Western India, to interfere in the carrying trade between places like Agra and Delhi, which ever since the opening of the East Indian Railway has been exclusively in its hands, yet the Government of India have recently given to one of its opponents the construction and working of the Agra-Delhi Chord.

It is suggested that these and similar questions are those to which the public of Calcutta should direct their best attention, realizing that their interests are identical with those of the East Indian Railway.

CHAPTER XX.

THIRD CLASS PASSENGERS.

THIRD class passengers constitute a very large proportion of the coaching traffic of the East Indian Railway; they provide nineteen-twentieths of the total passenger traffic and account for four-fifths of the coaching receipts. Recognising that the prosperity of the coaching traffic mainly depends upon its lowest class passengers, the attention of the Board of Directors and of the staff in India has always been directed towards measures for the development and convenience of this class.

In the year 1882, the third class fare had been reduced under the directions of the Board from 3 to $2\frac{1}{2}$ pies, or to, say, one-fifth of a penny per mile, but the question of making a further reduction in the charge was, from the time of his appointment as Chairman, constantly in the mind of General Sir Richard Strachey; unfortunately there were considerations that necessitated delay in carrying out his views; nothing could be done before the railway was prepared with additional rolling-stock, and it was on this account alone that concessions had to be given cautiously.

Addressing the shareholders in June 1894, General Sir Richard Strachey remarked: "The measures now being taken for providing a substantial increase to the passenger vehicles will, I hope, soon admit of some modifications of the fares of the lowest class, that will extend the facilities for travelling to a larger proportion of the population, for no proposal for any reduction of these fares could be practically entertained until the available rolling-stock was sufficient in quantity to meet a considerable increase of numbers, which at present is far from being the case." And again in December 1897 : "That there is still a very large field for the profitable development of the third class traffic is beyond question, but it could not be fully realized without a further reduction of rates, which the Board would not hesitate to introduce under suitable arrangements, one essential preliminary step being the construction of a large additional number of vehicles, without which it would be impossible to cope with the increased traffic that must be anticipated. The Board continue to keep this subject in view, and generally are increasing the facilities for travelling." In 1900 proposals for reducing the passenger fares were still under consideration, and in 1901 the first step was taken. In his Address to the shareholders in 1901, General Strachey said: "The Board have still been unable to carry out any general reduction of the passenger fares such as

they would desire to adopt, from their inability to provide the additional carriages, without which this could not be undertaken, but a small advance in this direction has been made by reducing the rates for long distances."
In his Address in December 1904, General Strachey remarked in regard to the third class: "With a view to stimulating the chief branch of the traffic, the Board have taken steps for a further reduction of third class fares for distances above 100 miles, and are prepared to carry out further reductions when proper provision is made for the addition to the carriage stock, which, it may be presumed, will be necessary to meet the requirements of the increased traffic likely to follow the reduction of fares."

The reduction in third class fares referred to was, like the coal rates, based on a sliding scale, according to the length of journey made.

For the first 100 miles the fare of $2\frac{1}{2}$ pies per mile remained as at present, the scale for longer distances being, on the additional length travelled—

    101 to 300 miles, 2 pies per mile,
    over   300 miles, $1\frac{1}{2}$ pie ,,   ,,

Further reductions will probably be made on the same basis of a sliding scale, and may be looked for as soon as the railway is better equipped with coaching stock. Up to the present additions to the rolling stock have barely kept pace with the normal growth of the traffic. The East Indian Railway has never been ahead of requirements, it has never had a margin to meet any large accession of passengers, and during times of pressure third class carriages have to be supplemented by goods wagons; this state of affairs is most undesirable, but it is obvious that, unless large additions are made to the coaching stock, it must either continue or passengers be turned away.

Apart from the consideration of the question in England, in India also the third class passenger has had constant attention. As far back as 1893 there was much controversy on a proposal made by the late Mr. Horace Bell, then Consulting Engineer to the Government of India, that a very sweeping reduction in the fare of the lowest class should be made. Mr. Bell proposed a fare of $1\frac{1}{2}$ pie per mile, but his proposal met with little or no acceptance; it was rejected by the Director-General of Railways, by the President of the Railway Conference, and by several managements, who all considered it not only Utopian but impossible. Beyond this was the fact that the third class passenger traffic was rapidly growing under the tariff introduced in 1882, and that a $1\frac{1}{2}$ pie rate tried on the Madras Railway had proved a failure.

It must never be forgotten, however, that India is a country of poor people and that when the average wage of the population is considered, in relation to the fares now charged, it means that only about 21 miles can be travelled for an average day's earnings. In America the third class passenger can travel about 60 miles for a day's wage, and in England about 40 miles. Therefore the fares in India should be as low as they can possibly be made, and in time it is hoped that material reduction will be possible.

Taking periods of 5 years from 1882, the following figures shew the number of third class passengers carried and the earnings therefrom on the East Indian Railway system :—

Year.	No.	Rs.	
1882	9,066,953	99,99,999	E. I. Proper.
1887	12,118,381	107,85,077	do.
1892	14,662,138	124,40,358	E. I. Ry. System.
1897	15,776,104	132,46,810	do.
1902	19,845,498	155,61,674	do.
1905	22,126,477	172,45,816	do.

Besides reductions in fares charged, other steps have from time to time been taken towards improving the facilities for travelling in the third class. In 1897, under the direct orders of the Chairman, the mail trains were thrown open to third class passengers; previous to this the main line mail trains below Allahabad only carried higher class passengers, and their servants. Then again the type of carriage has been greatly improved, separate vehicles have been provided for women, and lavatories are a feature of present day stock. Beyond this, the train service has been greatly added to and accelerated, but still it is quite admitted that a good deal remains to be done. In 1904 the Government of India invited railway servants to write essays, suggesting measures likely to ameliorate the conditions of travel, and to deal generally with the wants of third class passengers, showing how they could best be met. These essays gave food for thought to many railway employés, and several valuable suggestions were made which it is hoped will in time bear fruit. On the East Indian Railway an express train for lower class passengers has recently been introduced and is now one of the most popular and remunerative long distance trains run over the line, and it is now being considered whether a second similar train cannot be run.

CHAPTER XXI.

Proposed Central Station in Calcutta.

In a previous chapter reference has been made to a proposal, made in 1862, to bridge the Hooghly River, as near as possible to Calcutta, and to construct in the metropolis a central terminal station, so as to form a more perfect connection between the railway and the capital, and to afford the public a more convenient point for taking or leaving the rail. In those days there was no bridge of any kind across the river, and passengers and goods had to be boated or ferried over the Hooghly, to and from the railway station, an arrangement so inconvenient as to be more easily imagined than described; it was then indeed a pilgrimage to get to or from the East Indian Railway Station at Howrah.

Since then a floating road bridge has been constructed and it is as easy to approach Howrah Station from say, Chowringhi, as it is to drive from Oxford Circus to Waterloo. But it is not the passengers or goods from Chowringhi who need to be considered; they are in the minority, and it makes little difference to them whether the railway station is in Howrah or in Dalhousie

Square or in Bow Bazaar. The mass of the people, the great native population of Calcutta, live on the North side of the city, and for these Howrah is just as conveniently situated, as it would be if the site was fixed in the centre of the business part of the town.

In 1899, however, the idea of constructing a central station in Calcutta, which for some years had remained dormant, was revived. Proposals were made by a Syndicate known as the "Calcutta Central Railway Syndicate," and their proposals were considered by a committee and ultimately by the Government of India.

Briefly stated the Syndicate offered to construct a bridge, with a central railway and a central station, at an estimated cost of 425 lakhs of rupees, accepting a guarantee of $2\frac{1}{2}$ per cent on the capital employed, the revenue to be derived from a toll on goods and passengers.

The Committee who investigated the proposal agreed that a central railway station was preferable to maintaining different termini on the margin of the town; they agreed that Bow Bazaar afforded the best site; they thought however that the expense should not be defrayed in the manner proposed by the Syndicate, by the levy of tolls, but that the construction should be undertaken by the railways concerned, and not by a separate Company. While they considered it desirable to construct a railway bridge over the Hooghly, and to connect the railways on the West and East banks, by a line running through the heart of the city, their approval was subject to the condition that the scheme was financially practicable.

On the question of the estimated cost and of the possible revenue there was much difference of opinion, and ultimately the Government of India informed the Syndicate that their offer, unsupported as it was by those most interested, namely, the public of Calcutta, could not be entertained.

In the meantime the Lieutenant-Governor of Bengal, who had given the question his most careful consideration, made a counter-proposal "to develop the use of Sealdah," the terminus of the Eastern Bengal State Railway on the Eastern border of the city, "as a passenger station for the traffic with Upper India and for lessening the concentration of traffic at Howrah by every practicable means."

His views were summarized in these terms:

(1) "A railway bridge below Naihati is not at present required; when one is required it should not be built below Cossipore. The construction of any bridge on piers in the stream, at or near Howrah (whether road or railway bridge), would be an experiment so dangerous to the shipping interests of the port that it would not be justified, unless traffic could be served by no other reasonable alternative."

(2) The plans for railways from West and North-West of Calcutta should be prepared with this in view.

(3) The development of goods traffic, *viâ* the Jubilee Bridge, to and from the Kidderpore Docks, for both exports and imports, should be encouraged by all reasonable and practical means.

(4) The use of Sealdah as a passenger station from and to Upper India should be carefully developed and all concentration of traffic at Howrah, passenger or goods, lessened by every practical means.

(5) Another and more central railway station in the heart of Calcutta is not required, would add to the grave congestion of the area, and could not be made remunerative.

With a good deal of this the Board of the East Indian Railway concurred. They agreed that a railway bridge below Hooghly was not needed; stated that they had done and would always do all in their power to develop and encourage goods traffic *viâ* the Hooghly Bridge, by equalizing the rates on all traffic passing from any part of the East Indian Railway, to and from the Docks, with those to and from Howrah; though the distance from Hooghly to the Docks is about 12 miles greater than to Howrah, and though the capital expenditure on the Hooghly Bridge and its approaches and subsidiary stations had amounted to between 60 and 70 lakhs of rupees. They had, they said, in order to facilitate the passage of export traffic, pressed on the Government of India the necessity for allowing the East Indian Railway to construct a separate line of its own from the Hooghly Bridge to the Docks.

As to the use of Sealdah as a passenger station the Board remarked that in their view "the character of the passenger traffic that is now dealt with at Howrah cannot be properly understood, if it is supposed that it has reached its present development from any causes other than those arising from the necessities of the case, and the natural adaptation of the population of Calcutta and the suburban towns, under the conditions of their various occupations and habits of life, to the conveniences offered to them by the railway. It cannot be doubted that during the fifty years and upwards, during which the Howrah Station had formed the principal terminus of the East Indian Railway, the population has settled itself locally, with an intelligent appreciation of the best means of obtaining the services of the railway in the form most likely to be advantageous to it."

The Board, however, were in no way averse to the use of Sealdah as a supplementary station to Howrah, they had in fact made a proposal to this effect some years previously. They desired an experiment to be made by starting at least one East Indian Railway passenger train from Sealdah instead of from Howrah, but circumstances prevented the trial, and it is remarkable that there has never been any public expression, on the part of any section of the Calcutta population, of the need of a direct train service from Sealdah to stations on the East Indian Railway.

The Board quite concurred with the view of the Lieutenant-Governor of Bengal that a central station was not needed. Calcutta is an essentially *terminal* station for all the railways that centre there, and no such transfer of passenger or goods traffic from station to station takes place in Calcutta, with a view to subsequent transmission over other lines, as is often the case at other large centres of population at which railway junctions take place.

There is in fact no valid reason for "a common passenger station for all lines centering in Calcutta," and though a central station and a railway bridge connecting Howrah and Calcutta would undoubtedly be a convenience, the cost of providing it is far too great to bring it within practicable reach.

What is wanted is a suitable and commodious station at Howrah, and this at last is being constructed, though, unfortunately, the Government of India have only sanctioned part of what the East Indian Railway originally proposed, as necessary to meet the joint requirements of themselves and of the Bengal-Nagpur Railway Company.

CHAPTER XXII.

Provident Institution.

The establishment of the East Indian Railway Provident Institution was the outcome of a desire, on the part of the Board of Directors, to assist their employés to make some provision for the period of their old age after retirement from the service, or for their families in the event of their premature death, and in a general way it followed the idea of the Superannuation Funds connected with the various English Railways.

The Institution was formally inaugurated with effect from 1st January 1868 and from that date membership was made a condition of service, men already in the service being allowed the option of joining or not, as they pleased. In the first instance the membership consisted of two classes—A and B—the one representing employés of European domicile and the other those representing other classes of employés drawing salaries of not less than Rs. 30 per mensem. The subscriptions were 5 per cent and $2\frac{1}{2}$ per cent of salaries respectively, and the Company undertook to add annual contributions thereto, provided the annual net earnings attained a certain limit, such contributions being distributed to members in proportion to the *total* amount standing at their credit on the books. The anticipations as to the net earnings of the railway were not realized at the outset, and it was not until 1874—the year of the Tirhoot Famine—that the first contributions were received. In the meantime, the disappointment referred to had led to considerable dissatisfaction amongst the staff, and in consequence of representations made to them the Board of Directors allowed all members the option of withdrawing from the Fund. This was availed of to a large extent, but with the prosperous outlook in 1874 there was a general desire for admission to the Fund, both on the part of those who had previously withdrawn from it and of others who had throughout refrained from exercising their option of joining, and in August 1874 the Board of Directors, as an act of grace, again threw open the door of admission to all who were eligible under the rules, reserving only the condition, that such option must then be exercised once for all and adding as a further concession that all members might subscribe as from 1st January 1874, in order to participate in the expected contribution for that year. This act of grace resulted in a large accession to the membership of the Fund and as it was immediately followed by a contribution equivalent to 87 per cent. of the total amount at credit of each member on the books on 31st December 1874, there was a universal feeling of gratification throughout the service, more especially among those members who had adhered to the Fund from the date of its inception and whose tenacity and loyalty were thus so substantially and unexpectedly rewarded.

The position continued in this state until 1880 when the first contract of the undertaking expired, and the then Agent, Sir Bradford Leslie, represented that the division of the membership into two classes and the limitation of subscriptions to salaries of not less than Rs. 30 per mensem created an undesirable distinction, which pressed hardly upon a large body of the Company's employés This representation was accepted by the Board of Directors, and from 1st January 1881, the previous class distinctions were abolished, and membership was eligible to all employés drawing a monthly salary of Rs. 15 and upwards, the general rate of subscription being fixed at 5 per cent. This rate was made compulsory, and as a further incentive to thrift, each member was permitted to add an additional subscription limited to a maximum of a further 5 per cent on salary, such optional subscriptions ranking for participation in the contributions by the undertaking—which at this time were declared half-yearly instead of annually as before—to the extent of the available surplus after all *compulsory* subscriptions had been credited a sum equivalent to cent. per cent. thereon.

The introduction of these new rules involved the division of contributions on the sum of the annual subscriptions, instead of, as heretofore, on the sum of the gross holdings of members, thus placing old and new members on the same footing, without regard to length of service and accumulations in the Fund. This action was resented by a large body of the older members whose profits were thereby considerably diminished. The opinion of Actuaries was taken, and after a full consideration of the case of the older members, the Board accepted the view that their legal rights had been to some extent invaded and allowed them a grant of Rs. 1,50,000 as compensation.

From this time—1st January 1881 to 30th June 1903—the annual contributions by the undertaking admitted of the addition to members' accounts, of sums equivalent to their annual subscriptions and a further considerable addition in respect of *optional* subscriptions.

In the meantime, some other Indian railways had adopted a fixed compulsory rate of subscription of $8\frac{1}{3}$ per cent. of salary ; optional subscriptions being at the same time permissible, practically without limit, up to the extent of salary, but debarred from participation in any share of the contributions, and it was found, on studying the cases referred to, that the basis of contribution, if authorized for adoption on the East Indian Railway, would admit of larger contributions, even though the actual amount of monthly subscriptions were reduced from 10 to $8\frac{1}{3}$ per cent. On a representation of the circumstances, the Board of Directors and the Secretary of State for India sanctioned the application of these new rules to the East Indian Railway, and they were accordingly adopted with effect from 1st July 1903 ; the result to members who accepted them being that they have since that date received as an annual contribution to their assets in the Fund a sum exactly equivalent to one month's pay—neither more nor less—and with the growing prosperity of the East Indian Railway undertaking there seems to be every prospect of this state of things being prolonged indefinitely.

No statement of the history of the East Indian Railway Provident Institution would be complete which omitted mention of the fact that it has already proved an invaluable boon to hundreds of retired East Indian Railway employés and their families, and that it deserves the fullest and most grateful recognition on the part of those who may confidently look forward to the benefits which it ensures on retirement. Still it does not do to trust to the Provident Fund alone as a *sufficient* provision for the future, especially in the case of those who retire out of India, and many hold that something more is needed to put railway servants on a par with those who retire from Government service on a pension.

CHAPTER XXIII.

HILL SCHOOL.

On the purchase of the undertaking by Government on 1st January, 1880, it was, as already explained, found that a sum of over four lakhs of rupees remained at credit of the Saving Bank and Fine Funds; the former representing profits on working and the latter the unexpended accumulations of fines levied from the staff. It was at once recognized that these monies should, if practicable, be devoted to some object for the benefit of the staff, and there was little difficulty in arriving at a unanimous decision, that the best means of securing this object was the provision of a school, in a temperate climate, for the education of the children of the European and Eurasian employés. The Company had already provided and subsidised schools at each of the large stations in the plains, both for the domiciled and the native staff, but there was a demand, on the part of the former class, for the benefits of a Hill climate for their children during the hot season and the question was how this demand could best be met. On the one hand, there were existing scholastic institutions at such of the Hill stations as Darjeeling, Mussoorie, Naini Tal,

Murree, and Simla which might have served the purpose, but either the character of endowments, or the scale of fees levied, debarred the larger proportion of the servants of the Company from obtaining the advantage of these schools and it was felt that the only feasible arrangement was to secure a purely railway school, under the absolute control of the principal officers of the Company. The results obtained by the North-Western (State) Railway from an experiment made in this direction at "Fairlawn" near Jherapani, a place situated about mid-way between Rajpore and Mussoorie naturally attracted enquiries to that locality, and it happened at this juncture that "Oakgrove," a wellwooded and secluded estate, comprising 193 acres of land in the adjoining vicinity, was in the market. This was purchased by the Company for the comparatively small sum of Rs. 30,000 and arrangements were at once made for erecting the requisite buildings. In June 1888, the school was opened with a capacity for 210 pupils, having cost with the estate a sum of Rs. 200,000. The Board having, at the outset, recognized the disabilities under which the staff lay in respect of the scale of fees charged by other available institutions decided to set apart a further sum of Rs. 200,000 as an endowment towards payment of the Teaching Staff, the one object kept permanently in view being that the scale of fees levied should be such that all members of the staff could avail themselves of the benefits of the school. On these grounds the scale was fixed at Rs. 14 for the first child, Rs. 12 for the second and Rs. 10 for the third and other children per mensem, a rate which, apart from the endowment and such grants-in-aid as could be obtained from Government, was obviously inadequate to cover the actual expenditure. This feature of the scheme, though not ventilated by the Committee of Management, was apparently recognized at the commencement by the staff, and many of the better-paid subordinate officers declined to send their children to the school and mainly, it is believed, owing to this fact the numbers of the scholars did not equal the capacity of the school until 1895. At this period applications exceeded the limits, and as there was still a balance of about a lakh of rupees remaining from the funds before mentioned, it was decided to purchase the adjoining "Jherapani" estate and build a separate school for girls on the site. This estate, comprising 52 acres of land, lies contiguous to the "Oakgrove" estate without any intervening boundaries, and on a favourable site on it, a well-built school for girls was erected, capable of accommodating 140 scholars, and opened in the month of April 1897. The total expenditure on the entire school, including the Hospital and Sanitarium, Swimming Bath and Bakery having cost Rs. 500,000 including the endowment.

On the whole, the school has proved an unqualified success, and in 1905 had an average resident attendance of 394 pupils. (There are no day scholars.) The accommodation, although stated generally at 210 in the boys and 140 in the girls' school, is fully equal to providing for 400 scholars without infringing the Government standard requirements in respect of the space necessary for each scholar unit.

With the advent of the East Indian Railway School at "Oakgrove" the North-Western Railway decided to close their adjacent establishment at "Fairlawn" and entered into an arrangement with the East Indian Railway Company: under it they secured the right to send the children of North-Western Railway employés to the school, and agreed in view of the fact that it had been erected, equipped and endowed from East Indian Railway sources, to guarantee a minimum sum per annum and the payment of a capitation fee that was mutually agreed upon as fairly representing the actual rate of expenditure unit, the North-Western Railway employé being only charged a sum relative to his salary and the difference made up from the revenue of the North-Western Railway. This arrangement has continued up to the present time, and has been found of mutual benefit to the school and the North-Western Railway employés.

With the expiration of the second contract between the Secretary of State for India and the East Indian Railway Company on 31st December 1899, the former secured to Government under the third contract all proprietary rights in the school, but left the control and management of it to the Company.

For some years past, the school attendance has, roughly speaking, been made up of an equal number of East Indian and North-Western Railway children, and lately two officers of the North-Western Railway have been, at the instance of the East Indian Railway Board of Directors, added to the list of *ex-officio* Governors of the school.

The standard of education at the school has been well maintained throughout. The pupils have taken a high place, and on more than one occasion the *first* place on the Government examination lists for the whole of the United Provinces. The same may also be said of the examinations for entrance to the Roorkee Engineering College. A large percentage of the ex-pupils have found situations on the parent lines which they represent, and have thus fulfilled the objects for which the school was established. Standing as it does at an elevation of 5,300 feet above sea-level the climate of the school is temperate: the site is salubrious and far from all insanitation, the entire estate being absolutely reserved for the purposes of the school. There is an excellent and pure water-supply flowing directly to the school, through its iron pipes, direct from the "Mossy Falls" springs.

There is a rifle-range and ample room for out-door games, which are marked features of the school course, and a large swimming bath.

In every way the school is simply but thoroughly equipped, and the Institution as a whole and the results obtained from it, form a most gratifying vindication of the impulse which led to its inception and of the expenditure of the large sum of money which it has entailed.

The constant aim of the governing body is not only to conserve, but, wherever possible, to increase, the benefits conferred by the Institution, the most recent addition being the grant by the East Indian Railway and North-Western Railway undertakings of Rs. 5,000 each per annum towards the foundation of scholarships and exhibitions, tenable by the pupils of the school.

CHAPTER XXIV.

GENERAL GROWTH OF TRAFFIC.

In the year 1889 the total receipts from all sources of traffic amounted to Rs. 458,79,405; in 1894 they were Rs. 543,33,171; by 1899 they had gone up to Rs. 655,07,440, and during 1905 they were no less than Rs. 779,45,988.

In 1889 the percentage of working expenses to gross receipts were 34·63, in 1894 30·64, in 1899 32·52, and in 1905 35·31.

Nothing could speak more eloquently than these figures of the management of the East Indian Railway; with a great expansion of traffic there has continued a marked economy in working, and it was this result that General Sir Richard Strachey set himself to achieve from the moment he assumed the Chairmanship. Addressing the shareholders in 1890, he said: "It was my aim, while in India to inculcate the absolute necessity for seeking better results.............so that while the greatest practical economy was ensured, the varied interests, connected both with the passenger and goods service of the railway, should be constantly respected and their reasonable demands complied with." Eight years later he comments on what had by then been accomplished in the following terms:— "The careful attention given to administrative measures has reduced the working expenses below the amount at which they stood twelve years ago, although the passenger traffic has increased more than 75 per cent. and the goods traffic nearly 50 per cent., and it may confidently be affirmed that this has been accomplished in conjunction with a greatly improved condition of the permanent way, works and rolling stock, and increased efficiency in every branch of the service."

The exceptional position of the East Indian Railway Company in relation to other Indian Railways and the economical way in which it is worked, compared either with Indian or English lines, has often formed a theme of comment in Sir Richard Strachey's addresses to the shareholders, but we need only quote one instance here—in 1897 he said: "It will, I think, be useful again to point out, as I have done on former occasions, the relative great importance of the East Indian Railway, in respect of the traffic with which it has to deal, compared to other Indian Railways, and from which you will better be able to judge of the nature of the responsibility which the Company accepts with the management of the undertaking. During the last four months for which we have returns of the traffic, it appears that the gross receipts of the East Indian Railway, the length worked being 1,833 miles, amounted to 187½ lakhs of rupees. During the same period, the aggregate receipts of the Great Indian Peninsular, the Indian Midland, the Bombay and Baroda, the Rajputana-Malwa and Bengal-Nagpur Railways, the total length worked on which was 5,399 miles, amounted in all to 188¾ lakhs of rupees."

The traffic of the East Indian Railway has continued to give results immeasurably beyond that of any other railway in India, and although this is in a large degree due to the enormous coal traffic carried, still the expansion of other branches of traffic has also been very considerable. Allowing for variations in the wheat, grain and seed trade, due to the nature of the export demand or to famine or other cause, there has been continuous and marked development in practically all classes and kinds of traffic, and this is a most satisfactory feature, as it is on the growth of the general traffic, in all its branches, that the Company must rely for its continued progress and prosperity, rather than on the expansion of any particular items.

In the interval between the years 1895 and 1900, there were increases under the head of passengers amounting to two millions in number; under merchandise to a little more than one million tons; and under coal to more than two million tons, but, although it is necessary to found a review of the working of the railway upon figures indicating numbers of passengers and quantities of goods carried, as well as the amount of rupees earned and spent in the process, yet this does not truly indicate the value or importance of the work done by the railway for the country.

"To appreciate this," General Strachey remarked in 1901, "we must bear in mind the enormous advantages given a vast population, by the increasing facilities for travelling over great distances which otherwise would have been practically impossible. The extent of this convenience is indicated by the fact that in the past half-year more than eleven million persons have travelled on the railway, ten millions of whom were of the less affluent classes. Similar considerations apply to the effect produced on the trade and material progress of the country. The protection against the worst results of drought has been complete and could have been obtained by no other means. The facilities for the transport of goods over considerable distances must have increased the potential wealth of the people by several millions sterling yearly, through giving the means of carriage, at very low rates, and opening markets that would otherwise have been inaccessible, thus greatly stimulating and supporting internal as well as export trade."

The growth of traffic on the East Indian Railway has in a large measure been due to attention to detail, and to the means taken to stimulate the internal as well as the export trade of the country. Changes in the habits of the people have also had their effect on the traffic of the railway, or to put it in another way, the railway has enabled the population to adopt measures or to alter customs which, but for the railway, would never have been thought of. This we see in many directions, but to take one illustration only; in the early eighties vegetable oil, locally manufactured, was the only illuminant used by the masses; a wagon load of kerosene oil was unknown, and only a few cases, for the use of Europeans and the more wealthy natives, were carried. Railway rates were reduced, and in 1889 the East Indian railway carried a traffic of 24,376 tons—further reduction followed and, in 1905, the year's traffic in kerosene oil amounted to no less than 88,751 tons, a considerable portion of which was carried in bulk, for the carriage of which the Company had in the meantime constructed special stock. Nowadays kerosene oil may be purchased in any village in India, and the people burn practically nothing else. Similar remarks might be made in respect to other details, and speaking of the great growth of traffic since the formation of the line, the money returns of the East Indian Railway having during 40 years increased more than a hundredfold, General Strachey remarked in 1896 " when it is remembered that the line with which we are concerned is no longer, as it was in 1855, the only, or almost the only, railway in India, but one out of many, we are enabled to form some idea of the great changes in the habits of the people, the surprising expansion of trade, the rapid development of the resources of the country and our immense strengthening of our hold of India which are due to the introduction of railways."

The following table shows the growth of traffic earnings, in periods of ten years, since the opening of the line :—

Gross earnings of the East Indian Railway system during the following years.

Period.	Coaching.	Goods and minerals.	Sundries.	Total.
	Rs.	Rs.	Rs	Rs.
15th August to 31st December 1854	87,962	3,551	1,767	93,280
1864	60,18,053	77,43,271	1,69,806	1,39,31,130
1874	88,48,497	2,70,77,403	14,12,461	3,73,38,361
1884	1,30,65,845	2,99,88,895	7,83,973	4,38,38,713
1894	1,81,50,604	3,53,55,879	8,26,688	5,43,33,171
1904	2,33,46,816	5,41,10,958	12,68,238	7,87,26,012

Number of passengers and tons of goods carried.

Period.	No. of passengers.	Tons of goods of all descriptions.
15th August to 31st December 1854	141,161	Not available.
1864	4,014,171	660,571
1874	6,038,191	2,330,907
1884	11,126,560	4,313,066
1894	17,269,825	6,133,732
1904	23,585,686	12,233,188

CHAPTER XXV.

Various Projects for dealing with the Export Coal Trade and other matters.

Mention has been made of a scheme to provide coal jetties and loading appliances at a point on the River Hooghly adjacent to the Botanical Gardens. The locality was considered eminently suitable and convenient for the purpose and the approach to it, from the vicinity of Bally Station, a short distance above Howrah, could, at the time it was mooted, have been constructed without interfering with valuable property, so that the expense was not likely to be unusually great. There was therefore some reason to hope that the Government would sanction the work, which, in the words of General Sir Richard Strachey, would "supply the coal owners of Bengal, the means of giving to the export trade a development commensurate with the almost inexhaustible supplies of the mineral which is within their reach and which it will be the endeavour of the undertaking to carry to the place of shipment at the lowest possible cost."

It was far from the object of the East Indian Railway, either in connection with *this* scheme, or other proposals put forward to assist the trade of Calcutta, to obtain any exclusive advantage for the Company, or to go in any way beyond the proper functions of a railway which, according to Sir Richard Strachey's policy, were "to extend to the utmost the means of transport for the commercial community generally, and to support, within the sphere of their legitimate action, all efforts made with this object, however they may originate." The scheme, if it had been adopted, would have assisted all railways bringing coal into Calcutta for export, but unfortunately differences of opinion arose as to the expediency of carrying out the proposal, and the idea was abandoned.

Later on another scheme was put forward, which may in fact be said to have been the revival, in another form, of a very old project. Colonel Gardiner, the Company's Agent in Calcutta, recommended the construction of a subsidiary port on the Mutlah River, at a place called Port Canning, to which a line of rail had already been constructed, and where it was thought that the export coal traffic could better be dealt with than at the Kidderpore Docks, which, it will be remembered, were originally intended for the export of grain and seeds but not of coal.

Surveys were made, and it was then found that the Mutlah had ceased to be a river in the ordinary sense of the term ; it had in fact become a tidal estuary or arm of the sea, with a very deteriorated channel, difficult to navigate. The conclusion come to was that the idea of establishing a coal export depôt at such a place failed to offer any prospects of success. This scheme also was abandoned.

Time went on, and the great growth of the coal export trade proved how necessary it was to afford some relief to the pressure on the resources of the docks. The Bengal-Nagpur Railway had not only gained access to the Jherriah field, but had extended their line *viâ* Midnapur to a point on the right bank of the Hooghly opposite Calcutta, immediately below the East Indian Railway Station of Howrah. Here they had established a wagon ferry, to get into direct communication with the Kidderpore Docks; in other words, a wagon loaded at any station on their system could be passed by their own route to the Kidderpore Docks without break of bulk. They also had access to the docks *viâ* Asansol and the Jubilee Bridge at Hooghly, but neither of these routes gave them all they wanted. They appeared to desire to wrest from the East Indian Railway the bulk of the coal export trade, by constructing a line to a point on the Hooghly some miles below Calcutta, where they proposed to establish docks, provided with mechanical loading appliances and to divert the coal export trade to this point. The *place* where it was proposed to place this coal export depôt was known as Luff Point, but in the opinion of those best acquainted with the river it was not possible to take ships in and out of docks at Luff Point with any degree of safety or without obstructing the navigation of the river. The Government, however, appointed a Commission to consider the scheme which involved many issues, as, for instance, the ability of the Kidderpore Docks to deal with the trade; the possible expansion of the coal export business of the port in the future ; the cost of constructing new docks and the difficulties of dealing with coal exports at a place distant from Calcutta, to which only one railway would have the means of approach.

The Commission met in Calcutta in the cold season of 1900-1 and went very fully into the subject, with the result that the scheme, as put forward by the Bengal-Nagpur Railway, was not accepted. Public opinion in Calcutta was divided, but in the main it was opposed to the idea. The "Englishman," in common with other papers, published articles and correspondence containing different views. The first of these, being a fair sample of the feeling at the time, is partly reproduced, and it will be noted that the policy suggested in this article is the solution ultimately come to, *viz.*, equal rates, by both the East Indian and Bengal-Nagpur Railways, from the Jherriah coalfield to Calcutta.

The Luff Point Scheme.

"The Luff Point Scheme is likely to develop into one of the most momentous economic problems ever placed before the Calcutta public, and it is well that its true issue and effect on the trade of the port be considered, before the Commission, which will shortly sit, begins to take evidence. A little more than two years have passed since the Government decided to give the Bengal-Nagpur Railway access to the Jherriah coalfields. The coal trade had pressed for the admission of this line, because it was felt that there would then arise a competition between the East Indian and Bengal-Nagpur Railways, and that as a result the freight on coal would be reduced, and beyond this it was thought that collieries would be put in a more favourable position in regard to wagon supply. The actual effect has been that the advent of the Bengal-Nagpur Railway has opened out a large additional area of supply, and this has helped materially to bring down the sale price of coal; whether colliery proprietors have really benefited is an open question, but at any rate they have attained their object. In giving the Bengal-Nagpur Railway access to the Jherriah field, the Government laid down as a principle that the collieries in the field, wherever situated, might call for the wagons of whichever of the two railways they desired to consign their coal by, and the railways decided that rates should be equal by both routes.

Recently the Government held that neither of the two railways, competing for the traffic under these conditions, should be allowed to go below the prescribed minimum rate of $\frac{1}{10}$th pie per maund per mile, and consequent on this decision the Bengal-Nagpur Railway, which, in some instances, had gone below the minimum, in order to equalize charges with the shorter route, viâ the East Indian Railway, enhanced its rates to the public, not as might have been expected to the minimum allowed, but in some cases to a great deal beyond. The effect has temporarily been to put the Bengal-Nagpur Railway out of competition for the carriage of the export trade, but we cannot think that the Government intended that this should be the sequence of their decision, and undoubtedly the position is capable of a simple solution, which neither the East Indian nor Bengal-Nagpur Railways could object to. And we should say that a solution is possible which would also be acceptable to the trade, who cannot expect more than that both railways should be placed on equal terms for their custom, and that, as a consequence, freight to Calcutta should not be higher, from any point by the longer route, than it is by the shorter.

We hold in fact that the position prior to the recent ruling of Government was a satisfactory one, both to the railways and to the trade. Now if this is accepted, the question to consider is, what the result would be if the Luff Point Scheme was adopted and the export trade was taken from the Kidderpur Docks to Luff Point. First of all we may assume that the Government would be bound to give the East Indian Railway access to Luff Point, on the same terms as the Bengal-Nagpur Railway. In other words, the East Indian Railway would be empowered to run coal to Luff Point at the same rate of freight as the Bengal-Nagpur Railway, and, so far as can be seen, over the same route as the Bengal-Nagpur Railway for most of the way. Were this not so, or, in other words, were the East Indian Railway put out of competition for the carriage of export coal, the trade would revert to much the same position as before the Bengal-Nagpur Railway was admitted to the Jherriah coal-field, that is to say, coal owners would again become dependent upon one line of railway for the carriage of their coal instead of two. Does the trade consider that they would be any better served by the Bengal-Nagpur Railway alone than they were previously served by the East Indian Railway alone? The Chairman of the Indian Mining Association proved beyond question, at a recent meeting, that the Kidderpur Docks were capable of dealing with any likely expansion of the coal trade for many years to come, and that Luff Point was not wanted. Why then saddle the port with costly facilities which are not required and which in the end the public must pay for ?

Luff Point is not wanted; what is wanted is already available, *viz.*, two railways between the coal-fields and the port of Calcutta. Beyond this, equal rates and facilities should be given by both railways, and no more money should be wasted on additional lines or docks; in saying this we include the costly Bankura-Bishenpur Chord Line Scheme. The accident that one railway happens to have a somewhat shorter route than the other should not, in a case of this kind, be allowed to influence the question of rates, so long as the percentage of difference in mileage is only nominal; and where the interests of both railways are identical with those of the trade, we may be confident that in no case would they charge anything beyond the lowest possible freight. If, however, one railway ran to Luff Point and the other to the docks and both charged, as they undoubtedly would, equal rates to either place, the trade would go to the point from which shipping charges were lowest, and in this case either Luff Point or the docks would be bound to become a white elephant, with which the port of Calcutta would be eternally saddled."

To go back a few years earlier than the Luff Point controversy. In 1898, in order to relieve the pressure on the East Indian Railway below Burdwan, where, whenever traffic was at all brisk, there was constant congestion, the Company proposed to construct a short chord to Howrah. The route was surveyed, but before sanctioning construction the Government appointed a Committee to consider its necessity.

This Committee sat in 1901, Mr. James Douglas, the Agent, representing the Railway Company, the rest of the Committee being composed of Public Works officers, the majority of whom were opposed to the scheme. Besides considering the measures necessary for the relief of congestion of traffic on the lower section of the East Indian Railway the Committee also dealt with the following questions :—

(1) The entrance of the Bengal-Nagpur Railway into the Jherriah coal-fields.

(2) The provision of an independent access to Calcutta from the North-Western Provinces.

As a result the short chord line proposed by the East Indian Railway was abandoned, and the Bengal-Nagpur Railway were allowed into Jherriah.

CHAPTER XXVI.

STATISTICS.

ACCURATE statistics of work done on Indian railways have, almost from the earliest days, been held to be one of the most important factors of economical management, as they afford an efficient means of ascertaining the work actually performed and the cost of performing it. The history of railway statistics in India is contained in a note published by General Sir Richard Strachey in 1901, here reproduced :—

"Note on the bearing of accurate statistics of working on the economical management of railways :—

"The *Times* of the 14th December, quoting from the *Statist* of the same date, which has a long article on the subject, announces, on the authority of the General Manager of the great railway system known as the North-Eastern Railway of England, as though it was something remarkable, that its managers have determined to adopt what the *Statist* calls the American system of ton and passenger mileage returns. It tells us also, on the same authority, what I think will startle some persons, that the average train loads on *the North-Eastern* system during the year

1900 were, in round numbers, in passenger trains only 62·4 persons, in merchandise trains only 44 tons, in mineral trains only 92½ tons, or in merchandise and minerals taken together 66·6 tons; and that the average rates charged were, for passengers ·617d. per mile, for merchandise 1·64 per ton per mile, and for minerals 1d. per ton per mile, or taking merchandise, live stock and minerals together 1·24 per ton per mile; and there is no reason to suppose that the train loads and charges on other great English lines differ materially from those of the North-Eastern.

Managers of Indian railways will fully understand from these figures how it is that English Companies with their constant increases of capital expenditure, in working expenses and in the ratio of expenses to receipts, and in demands made on them for reduction of rates, are beginning to find themselves on the edge of a precipice, with the greater part at least of the dividends on their ordinary stock in jeopardy.

But they might also say that the discovery of the value of ton and passenger mileage returns comes more than a little late, and that to speak of it as an American practice implies a curious ignorance that the practice, was adopted more than 30 years ago, under the orders of the Government of India, by all Indian railways, and its results for at *least* 25 years have been widely disseminated *in* innumerable copies of Indian half-yearly reports, many of which must, at some time or other, have been in the hands of the bulk of the Managers and Directors of English railways, if only because many of them hold Indian railway stock.

The present seems therefore a suitable occasion for stating the reasons which led to the adoption of these returns in India, and the results which have followed their introduction. I shall confine myself on this subject to the East Indian Railway, which took and has kept the lead in the matter from the first.

In the year 1867, thirteen years after the opening of the line, the Board of the East Indian Railway found themselves in a very serious condition. Their capital expenditure had long passed all expectations, demands for fresh and heavy expenditure were reaching them almost by every mail, their working expenses were high and their traffic was disappointingly small It was felt that something must be done and it was finally determined to despatch the gentleman who was then, and still is, their Consulting Engineer, Mr. as he was then, now Sir Alexander Rendel, to India to consult with the Company's officers there generally on the subject.

I was then Secretary of the Public Works Department of India, and naturally I saw a great deal of Mr. Rendel. Of the result of *his visit in* respect to capital expenditure, I need say nothing here, except that it was highly successful. But by far the more important result, for, in fact, the usefulness of the line to India, as well as its financial success, has been determined by it, was that our many conversations on the subject led to this conclusion—that nothing of value could be effected on Indian lines, until their traffics were stated in ton and passenger mileage. My own recollections of the details of our discussions are, from lapse of time, getting hazy; but Sir Alexander Rendel tells me that he well remembers how, when he expressed a doubt whether the Companies could be induced to prepare the necessary statements, I declared that "it could be done and should be done" and somehow or other done it was at once. The decision was come to in the early part of 1868. Of course, it took some little time to set things in motion; but very early in the seventies, Sir Juland Danvers, then the Government Director of Indian Railway Companies published, in his Annual report to the Secretary of State, a note by Mr. Rendel on the subject; and in 1874 the East Indian Railway Board took the matter up by publishing in their report for the second half of 1873, the statement (the form of which will be seen on page 234) then and long afterwards known as Mr. Rendel's statement, for the second halves of 1871, 1872 and 1873. This continued to the time when the Government of India took over from Sir Juland Danvers the duty of preparing the annual report on Indian railways, and developed their statistics into the perhaps over-elaborate form in which they are now drawn up. The Board from that time attached to their half-yearly reports, and still do so, a copy of so much of the Government statistics as included the more simple statement of their earlier reports.

It has, moreover, become the established practice to place, week by week, before the official meetings, at which are present the Agent and Heads of Departments, as well as the Government Consulting Engineer and Examiner of Accounts, a statement containing the principal results of the working, so that the whole of the officers concerned in the management of the traffic are kept continually informed of the progress made, and immediate attention is directed to any falling off or improvement in the train and wagon loads, as well as to the increases and decreases of the traffic of all descriptions and the receipts from it.

The practical results of this system, the influence of which on the Administrative Staff extends also to the Board of Directors, to whom these weekly statements are regularly submitted, may be gathered from the annexed comparison of the traffic of the line for the first half of 1872, before the new statistics had produced much, though *still some* result, with that of the first half of 1901—when they had been acted on for more than thirty years. I take for the former period what was then known as the main line. I omit the Jubbulpore line, the accounts of which were at the time stated separately, because it was then but new, and its union with the main line would lead to unduly unfavourable conclusions. I convert also rupees from their standard value in 1872 of 1s. 10d. to their present price of 1s. 4d. and I take a passenger train mile in both cases as costing the same as a goods train mile, and compute the cost per train mile in the same way as in 1872.

We have then the following :—

PASSENGER TRAFFIC.

	1st half year, 1872.	1st half year, 1901.
Miles open	1,281	2,136
1. Average receipts from each passenger train per mile	5s. 1·3d.	4s. 8·8d.
2. Average sum received for carrying a passenger (taking all classes together) one mile	·27d.	·223d.
3. Average number in any passenger train at any one time	235	257
4. Average cost of running a train one mile	2s. 3¼d.	1s. 10¾d.
5. Average cost of carrying a passenger one mile	·112d.	·088d.
6. Average profit on each passenger per mile	·158d.	·135d.
7. Average number of passenger trains running over each mile of line each way per diem (supposing all trains to run over the whole line in operation).	2·25	3·91
8. Average number of passengers passing over each mile of line both ways per diem	1,064	2,010

GOODS TRAFFIC.
(Including minerals.)

	1st half year, 1872.	1st half year, 1901.
Miles open	1,281	2,136
1. Average receipts from each goods train per mile	7s. 6d.	6s. 4d.
2. Average sum received for carrying one ton of goods (taking all classes together) one mile	·789d.	·377d.
3. Average load in tons in any goods train at any one time	tons 113·75	tons 201·59
4. Average cost of running a train one mile	2s. 3¼d.	1s. 10⅜d.
5. Average cost of carrying a ton of goods one mile	·238d.	·112d.
6. Average profit on each ton per mile	·551d.	·265d.
7. Average number of goods trains running over each mile of line, each way per diem (supposing all trains to run over the whole line in operation)	3·68	7
8. Average number of tons passing over each mile of line both ways per diem	tons 833·5	tons 2,820

The main features of this comparison are:—

1. The great increase of the average daily number of passengers and tons of goods passing over each line of railway, being for the former 100 per cent. and for the latter nearly 250 per cent., while the mileage worked has increased more than 50 per cent.

2. The increased train load of goods, which has been nearly doubled.

3. The reduced charge for goods, the average now being considerably less than *one half that of 1872.*

4. The reduction of the cost of running trains, amounting to about one-fourth.

Under the influence of steady attention to train load we first largely reduced the mileage cost of carrying a passenger or a ton of goods. Then, having reduced our expenses, we were enabled to reduce our rates; and then, by reducing our rates, we increased our traffic. We also saved in capital expenditure by reducing the quantity of rolling and locomotive stocks, and of station accommodation of all kinds, &c., &c., that was needed to meet the requirements of traffic.

The very different conditions of the two countries does not admit of any useful comparison of the money receipts and charges between the East Indian and North-Eastern Railways. As to train loads, however, it may be remarked that the passenger train loads, though four times those of the North-Eastern, are less than on several other Indian lines. The cause lies in our rates, which are still too high. In goods, although we have nearly doubled our train loads since 1872, the goods and mineral train loads should be greater than they are, and I have no doubt that a judicious reduction of rates would lead to an increase in quantities carried that would be profitable. There are, however, difficulties in the way of making provision for any considerable increase to traffic, whether in passengers or goods, that render any immediate action in this direction impracticable.

If it be asked what have ton and passenger mileage returns to do with all this, the reply is, that with ton and passenger mile returns, as well as passenger and goods train miles, you arrive at once at the average passenger and goods train loads, and these are a test of the healthy management of a line, such as a healthy pulse is to the human being. Making, of course, due allowances for variation of circumstances they are infallible. Low train loads, except under known or easily ascertainable circumstances point, without doubt, to faulty management. If uncorrected, they will lead a line to destruction, for low train loads mean high train mileage. The working expenses of a railway are not necessarily proportionate to the traffic carried, but to the effort made to carry the traffic—that is mainly to the train mileage run ; and a needlessly high train mileage means capital and revenue wasted in every possible form, and, worse than this, it means rates and fares beyond the necessities of the case and consequent needless burdens on commerce. The public always pays ultimately for the blunders of railway management.

We who are connected with India are free, at any rate to a great extent, from this reproach, but this is due, in a degree which possibly will never be fully admitted, to our ton and passenger mileage returns and the way they have been forced by the administrations on the attention of the Executives of Indian railways."

It will be noted that it took nearly thirty years to increase the loads of goods trains from 113·75 tons to 201·59 tons and that General Sir Richard Strachey was not altogether satisfied with the results. By 1902 the figure had gone up to 202·75 tons, but early in 1903 Sir Alexander Rendel once more visited India and attended one of the weekly official meetings at which the statistics are examined; he drew special attention to the subject of train loads and said that in his opinion the average weight in a train should be increased to 250 tons. Efforts were made to bring about the desired result, and what followed is within the knowledge of all interested in the subject; by the close of 1904, the average weight had not only been increased to the figure mentioned by Sir Alexander Rendel, but had gone beyond it, and has since risen to over 275 tons.

Statistics not only form the true basis for economies in working, but have enabled the East Indian Railway Company to initiate with confidence a liberal policy in regard to rates, and to introduce concessions which, in their absence, would be thought dangerously near the line where profit ends and loss begins. In the case of the East Indian Railway statistics have proved, not an end but a means to an end, and for their introduction and application to railway working in India, if not throughout the world, we have to thank General Sir Richard Strachey and Sir Alexander Rendel. As General Sir Richard Strachey said to the shareholders in 1898, statistics bring it within our reach to determine "how far the means employed are actually utilised, and in what direction waste occurs and where economy is to be sought for. I have no hesitation in saying that the unquestionably economical working of Indian railways generally, is in no small degree due to the system of check thus provided."

To further assist in raising the standard of work done, weekly statistics are now published shewing, for several sections of the line, the average load per wagon loaded on the district, the vehicle mileage, the up and down engine mileage, the engine hours, wagon miles per hour, train miles per hour and other details. This information is in the hands of the staff very shortly after the period to which it pertains, and is not only found a most useful record of work done in each district, but is a basis for discussion at the meetings of Traffic officers which are held every few months.

CHAPTER XXVII.

The Jamalpur Workshops.

It has often been asked why it was that Jamalpur was selected as the site for the Company's Locomotive Works. Jamalpur is off the main line, is distant from the Bengal coal-fields, whence not only its fuel but its pig iron has to be transported, and beyond this it has no natural water-supply.

To have selected such a place as the Head-Quarters of Locomotive Engineering works was obviously a blunder; as great a blunder perhaps as the construction of the tunnel near by, a piece of work that was altogether unnecessary and stands to this day a monument of the wasteful expenditure of the time. The chief reason for the choice seems to have been that Jamalpur was adjacent to the town of Monghyr, which had been known for years as the "Birmingham of the East," and it was conceived that a plentiful supply of skilled mechanics could always be drawn from that place. The inhabitants of Monghyr had for centuries been mechanics by trade, they were of a caste skilled in the manufacture of ironware, notably of guns, *pistols*, spears and other weapons, and were clearly the class of people who would readily take to mechanical engineering work.

Beyond this it must not be forgotten that, at the time the selection was made, Jamalpur was on, what was then intended to be, the main line of the railway.

Jamalpur was at first only an engine changing station, though light repairs were done in the running shed there. The actual head-quarters of the Locomotive Department were at Howrah, but this place, being near Calcutta, not only possessed great drawbacks but was too confined to admit of extensions. There was in fact no room in Howrah for the workshops of the Locomotive Department, as well as for the Company's Carriage and Wagon Building works, and after long and mature consideration it was decided to remove the former to Jamalpur. I am indebted to Mr. John Strachan, late Locomotive Superintendent of the Company, for the following account of the cause of the removal:—

"It was not till the early sixties that the late Mr. D. W. Campbell decided to remove the workshops to Jamalpur, and this was owing to the drivers and fitters giving trouble. They were all covenanted men from home who had left their families there, and as hotels and billiard rooms were their only amusement, it was no uncommon thing for men to leave the shops during working hours and adjourn to a hotel, then opposite the railway station, kept by a very civil old ship steward, named Bobby Deans, who could always give them something to eat, as well as something to drink and a game of billiards."

"There were also several other places of amusement in Howrah and Calcutta to which men could go, and among these was a place known as Wilson's Coffee Room."

"One day Mr. Campbell, returning from the weekly Meeting in the Agent's Office, happened to call at Wilson's Coffee Room for tiffin, and here he found three of his principal workshop foremen and two engine drivers enjoying themselves in rather a boisterous manner. They asked him to join them in having a peg. What he said in reply has never been recorded, but the men very quickly retired, and after that Mr. Campbell never rested until he had the workshops and Locomotive Offices removed from Howrah to Jamalpur."

It is no part of this history to trace the gradual growth of Jamalpur, from a small engine-changing station, to what is now known as the " Crewe of India," but the following account, kindly furnished me by Mr. A. P. M. Nash, of the Locomotive Department, is of undoubted interest, containing as it does a very clear description of Jamalpur and the Company's Works there at the present time.

"The supervising staff of the workshops consists of 26 Foremen and Assistant Foremen and about 180 European and East Indian mechanics; of the former a large proportion have been recruited from England direct. Practically the whole of this staff is housed in quarters owned by the Company, and live within easy distance of the workshops. Other buildings consist of a Church, Roman Catholic Chapel, Mechanics' Institute, Swimming Bath, Hospital, including a separate building for infectious diseases, and a School for the children of European and East Indian employés. There is also a Boarding-house in which 40 European and East Indian apprentices are lodged and cared for under the charge of a resident master and matron. In addition to this 21 live elsewhere in the station. It may perhaps not be out of place, while on this subject, to point out the importance of this system of training indentured apprentices. The recruitment of the subordinate supervising grade has hitherto been chiefly done by the introduction of men from England, but it is hoped that in the future suitable candidates will have been trained up in the workshops to take these appointments, and the expense of importing men will be saved, as well as the risk of the climate not suiting the men thus brought out to India for the first time. At the same time it must be remembered that an excellent field of employment is thus afforded for the sons of the Company's servants.

Jamalpur is the head-quarters of the East Indian Railway Volunteer Rifles, at the present time 2,300 strong, and the Armoury and Head-quarters staff are in Jamalpur.

The recreation of the men is not forgotten, and there is a flourishing Gymkhana in connection with the Mechanics' Institute, providing cricket, football, tennis, etc.

The workshops at the present time cover an area of about 100 acres, of which about 20 are roofed over, the whole being fenced in with a high iron fence. Fifteen years ago they occupied barely half of this space. At that time 3,122 men were employed compared with 9,428 this year (1906), the wages in 1890 amounted to Rs. 4,15,093 compared with Rs. 11,00,000 in 1905. The value of the outturn is about Rs. 54,00,000 a year or £360,000 compared with £58,332 in 1890. The above serves to give some idea of the vast strides that have been made in the last few years, and the growth of the Locomotive Department of the railway may also be gauged by the fact that in 1863 the total engine stock was 247, and at the present time is 952.

The shops are now or will be very shortly in a position to build locomotives to meet all the requirements of the line. The work of building locomotives has been actually going on for some years, but owing to the amount of repairs to existing stock that is necessary, new-engine building has had to be kept back. Almost all the parts of a locomotive can now be manufactured in the shops, including all steel castings, and the actual cost of a locomotive built at Jamalpur is therefore considerably less than one purchased and imported. The Jamalpur built engines have given most satisfactory results.

There are of course larger railway shops existing in Europe, but few are more self-contained or better equipped with modern electrically-driven machinery than these workshops. The distance from England and the cost of freight and the accompanying delays in complying with indents for materials, etc., have been successfully overcome by the liberal and progressive policy the Company have adopted in developing Jamalpur. It must not be overlooked that in addition to actual locomotive work, the workshops undertake work for the Engineering, Stores, Collieries and Carriage and Wagon Departments, the whole of the manufacture of the Denham & Olphert cast-iron sleeper, which is the standard in use on the line, being made here; the total value of the outturn for the Engineering Department in the half-year ending June 1905 being Rs. 10,77,375. All signalling and interlocking gear, posts, frames, etc., are manufactured complete, and this has become a very large item in the outturn, a more detailed description of which will be found below. It may truthfully be said that any general engineering work can be carried out in the shops, as occasion demands.

The question of the supply of native labour is now-a-days a serious one at Jamalpur, as the growth of the workshops has completely outgrown the local supply; it has therefore for some time past become necessary to bring in labour daily, from a distance of 19 miles on one side, 7 miles on another, as well as from Monghyr, the Civil Station, 6 miles distant. Workmen's trains are run out to these distances morning and evening to bring in and take back the workmen.

The water-supply of these large workshops is from time to time a source of anxiety. The daily consumption is about 350,000 gallons, and this is drawn from reservoirs in which rain water is stored, all available catchment area being " tapped " for the purpose ; the supply therefore is entirely dependent on the rainfall. For a period of two months or so, on two occasions during the last few years, due to a short rainfall, the reservoirs have become completely exhausted, and water has had to be brought in from the Ganges, 6 miles distant, in trains, and the shops thus kept in full work. This is a most expensive as well as unsatisfactory undertaking. It would seem that the only natural source from which a never-failing supply could be derived is the river Ganges at Monghyr, which is 6 miles distant.

The following is a list of the shops, with a brief description of certain of the most important :—

Steel Foundry.—The institution of a steel-making plant was due to the late Locomotive Superintendent of the Railway, Mr. A. W. Rendell, and was commenced in 1898. It then consisted of a 7-ton Siemens Martin open hearth furnace. Since then, at the suggestion of Mr. Tomyns R. Browne, the present Locomotive Superintendent, the furnace has been enlarged to a capacity of 10 tons, and a two-ton Tropenas converter plant has been added for small castings.

Iron Foundry.—This shop is probably one of the finest of its kind existing, covering as it does a floor area of nearly 100,000 square feet. The cupolas are charged from a bank, on which material is delivered in trucks on the same level as the charging doors. The average output of the foundry is 100 tons a day of finished castings. The pig iron used is chiefly from the Bengal Iron & Steel Company of Barakar. There are about 1,800 employés in this shop, of which a portion are coolie women.

Laboratory.—Close to the Foundries is situated the Laboratory, equipped with the necessary apparatus for determining the quality of metals and other materials, and their suitability for the purposes for which they are intended. The existence of the laboratory, under the supervision of a chemist and metallurgist, enables the manufacturing departments to be run on scientific and-up-to date lines.

Rolling Mill.—This shop was first started in 1879 and consisted of a 10-inch mill. Since then it has increased very considerably and now contains, in addition, a 12-inch and 14-inch mill, $3\frac{1}{2}$-ton steam hammer, a fishplate machine, and billet shears. Steam for driving the rolling mill engines is generated in boilers fixed on the top of the furnaces, and heated by the gases from the furnaces. The mill turns out the various sections of steel and iron rounds, channels, and angles required in the works, as well as fishplates. The outturn is about 400 tons a month.

Erecting and Fitting Shop.—This shop consists of three bays and a lean-to, each of a total length of 840 ft., and covering an area of 149,640 sq. ft. Two bays and the lean-to are occupied as erecting shops, while the third bay is used as a fitting shop. Each erecting shop bay is served with two electric overhead cranes of 30-ton capacity each, and the fitting shop with a 10-ton crane of same design. This shop is probably the finest erecting shop in existence.

Point Crossing and Signal and Interlocking Shop.—The work of constructing crossings and signals was first undertaken at Jamalpur in 1894, and at that time a small space of the tender shop was sufficient for its demands. Such was the rapid increase of this branch of work, that it very shortly necessitated the giving up of the whole of the tender shop, which had to be removed elsewhere. Lately another signal and interlocking shop has had to be added, and this branch is now equipped with its own machine tools, all operated by electricity, a small smithy with pneumatic hammers, etc. The output last year comprised 31 complete interlocking frames varying in size from 4 to 85 levers.

Machine Shops.—The work is divided into two sections, viz., general machine work, and locomotive machine work, each being accommodated in separate shops, the general machine shop covering a space of 49,950 square feet, and the other 51,615. As far as possible, the machines are grouped to avoid unnecessary handling of material, and to ensure a continuous sequence from roughing to finishing.

The other shops are as follows :—

Brass Foundry, Forge, Smithy, Pattern, Carpenter, Bolt and Nut, Brass Finishing, Tin and Coppersmiths', Cold Saw, Chain-testing, Wheel, Boiler, Millwright, Paint, and Tender Shop. In addition to which there is a large Detail Store.

I will conclude this chapter on Jamalpur by a brief description of the introduction of electricity into the workshops. The scheme for driving the workshops by electricity was first put forward when Mr. A. W. Rendell was Locomotive Superintendent, and the electric power house actually commenced work in 1901. It then consisted of three Belliss-Holmes direct-coupled sets, each of 100 Kilowatt output. The power house is situated centrally with a view to the most economic distribution of electric power to the various workshops. Later expansion has comprised the addition of a 300-kw. condensing turbo-generator of the Parson's type running at 3,000 revolutions per minute. The power is distributed to the shops from various service switch panels, which control the circuits going to the shops. The electrical energy conveyed to the shops is transformed into mechanical power by means of electric motors, which are in part arranged for driving machine tools, placed in convenient groups, and in part disposed for individual drives. There are some 25 electrically-operated cranes, ranging from 2 to 30 tons in lifting capacity, and the motor equipment of these, together with the remainder of the shop driving, comprise an aggregate of some 1,500 H.-P.

Steam at 150lb. pressure per square inch is furnished to the generators from a battery of fourteen boilers of the Babcock & Wilcox type, of which eight are hand and six are mechanically fired. Natural draught is furnished by two steel chimneys, each 120 feet high, having a clear diameter of 5 feet 6 inches. These chimneys were built at Jamalpur, and erected section by section.

The boundary of the workshops is lighted by means of arc lamps, worked from a Thomson-Houston series arc light machine, which in turn is driven by a direct-coupled electric motor. An electricity supply to the greater part of the Company's houses and buildings, including the Mechanics' Institute, is afforded from the power house. Current for fans and lights in the buildings is supplied from a ring main, fed at suitable points by service feeders. The ring main is supplied automatically at constant pressure by means of a specially-designed Booster. The distributing network consists of bare copper aerial conductors, carried on steel poles, about 25 feet above ground level. Each house is furnished with an electricity meter. The provision of electric fans and lights adds very considerably to the comfort and welfare of the occupants of the houses during the hot weather.

Much might be said concerning the sanitation of the station, suffice to say it is considered the model Municipality of Bengal."

CHAPTER XXVIII.

OUTBREAK OF PLAGUE—IMMUNITY OF E. I. R. FROM SERIOUS ACCIDENTS—THE DELHI DURBAR—MR. T. ROBERTSON'S ENQUIRY INTO INDIAN RAILWAY WORKING—REMOVAL OF CARRIAGE SHOPS TO LILLOOAH.

IN May 1898 plague first appeared in Calcutta, and a great panic among the native population of the city and suburbs followed. This panic was not caused so much by a fear of the disease itself as by a fear of the sanitary precautions which it rendered necessary. The precautions entailed much that was repugnant to the habits and feelings of the people of India, and extreme terror fell upon the lower classes of the native community, apparently due to exaggerated and absurd rumours about the nature and stringency of the precautionary measures to be taken; rumours originating partly in ignorance and partly perhaps in malice. Shortly after the first outbreak in the metropolis, forty thousand terror-stricken persons left Calcutta, within a few days, by the East Indian Railway alone; many fled from the city by other routes. As a result no boatmen, carters nor coolies were procurable, and at one time over 1,100 wagons of merchandize stood under load at Howrah, because of the impossibility of procuring labour to discharge them. It speaks well for the loyalty and devotion to duty of the subordinate Railway Staff that not a single man left his post, though many succumbed to the disease, and there were outside agitators trying their utmost to provoke a strike. Various means have been adopted by the Government of India to prevent the spread of plague and to stamp it out, but so far these have met with little success. For some years all railway passengers were subjected to medical examination at different stations on the line, where plague camps were established, but this system effected no good and was most unpopular, so was abandoned. Plague has in fact unfortunately continued in India since 1898 to the present day, and unhappily there are as yet no indications of its disappearing.

The East Indian Railway has been remarkably immune from accident, but one of the most extraordinary occurred on the 29th of June 1902. A mixed train proceeding *viâ* the loop line was blown over by a tornado in the vicinity of Rampore Hât Station and thirteen passengers were killed and fifteen wounded. That the number was not far greater, seeing that practically the whole train was wrecked and that there were some 300 passengers in it, was due to the fact that the wind brought the engine to a stand before the vehicles were overthrown. Strange to say a very similar accident had occurred on the East Indian Railway some thirty years previously and very near the same place; in both cases the surrounding country was an open plain, the lines of the railway being laid on a slight embankment, about five feet high, with nothing whatever to break the force of the wind. Both these accidents were what is termed "acts of God"; serious accidents due to negligence or carelessness on the part of the staff have been rare and when they have occurred, there has fortunately been but little loss of life. Seeing that until very recently all points were worked by menials, there being practically no interlocking, this speaks well for the native staff.

In January 1903 a grand Durbar was held in Delhi in honour of the Coronation of His Majesty the King-Emperor of India. It was in November 1901 that the intention to hold an Imperial Durbar was first publicly announced, the railway had therefore little more than a year in which to prepare for the great accession of traffic it would have to carry in connection. The Delhi Station had to be completely remodelled, subsidiary lines and stations in the vicinity had to be constructed, the coaching stock, particularly the higher class, had to be augmented, the staff strengthened, their accommodation arranged for, and many questions of detail had to be worked out and settled beforehand. The East Indian Railway had often felt the strain of a heavy goods traffic; on this occasion the experience was to be of a totally different character, for though it is true that the rush of goods to Delhi before the Durbar caused a block, which there was considerable difficulty in clearing, the real difficulty was to provide stock in which to carry the higher class passengers, all of whom wanted to arrive and leave at the same time. To give some idea of the passenger traffic, it may be mentioned that in an ordinary month about four hundred first and second class passengers are carried by the East Indian Railway to Delhi; during the Durbar over twelve thousand had to be conveyed there within a few days, while the stock available was little more than sufficient to meet ordinary requirements. Fortunately a solution of the problem occurred to Mr. W. A. Dring, the General Traffic Manager. There were ready at the time the Durbar was announced, some bogie frames intended for the construction of lower class stock, and it was decided to alter certain of these for temporary use as sleeping cars, for higher class passengers. This step saved the situation. Had no additional stock been arranged for, it would have been impossible to deal with the traffic; practically no carriages could be hired from other railways, all were too busy themselves to lend any to the East Indian, and it was on the East Indian that the heaviest strain fell. The *Englishman* newspaper gauged the difficulty in a leader published on the 1st December 1902, and the following extract is taken from it :—

"The forthcoming Durbar at Delhi will be the biggest thing of its kind that India has ever seen. It will be attended by His Excellency the Viceroy, H. R. H. the Duke of Connaught and seventeen Governors, Lieutenant-Governors, Residents and Agents to the Governor-General, Chief Commissioners and other high British officials, fifty-four ruling Chiefs invited by His Excellency the Viceroy, and fifty ruling chiefs invited by Local Governments and Administrations, in addition to numerous titled native gentlemen and crowds of European guests and visitors from all parts of India. Most of the notabilities require special trains, many of them also require special trains for their guests and followers, and nearly everyone else wants special accommodation of some kind or another. Besides this the traffic in tents, camp equipage, horses and carriage will be immense, while the large army collected in Delhi and the vicinity means the transport by railway of vast supplies of all sorts. The magnitude of the traffic can hardly be appreciated, and seeing that a large proportion has to be carried over a lead of many hundred miles, it is not surprising that the Indian railways are confronted with difficulties and find it impossible to avoid congestion."

In his Report on the Durbar traffic the Officiating General Traffic Manager remarked :—

"It is hardly necessary to say that the Durbar traffic was unique and without precedent in Indian Railway working, for the Durbar of 1877 bears no comparison with it. It was recognised from the first that we had before us a task bristling with difficulties, and that the special class of traffic we would have to deal with would strain our resources to the utmost."

That all obstacles were overcome in the end without any serious hitch and without a single accident of any kind was more attributable to the personal exertions of the staff than to any facilities that were, or could possibly be afforded for the purpose. Crowding and some delay were inevitable, and the difficulty of preventing these was enhanced by the awkward and confined situation of the Delhi main station, into which most of the traffic had perforce to be brought.

One great result of the Durbar was that the remodelling of Delhi Station, which had long been contemplated, was materially hastened, while many lessons were learnt which should prove useful on a future occasion of a similar kind ; but it is evident that Indian Railways, having ordinarily but a comparatively very small upper class traffic to convey, will never be in a position to meet a great demand of this nature without difficulty. Commenting on the Durbar traffic General Sir Richard Strachey said to the shareholders :—

"The general effect of the great assemblage at Delhi on the traffic has been of doubtful advantage, the benefit derived from the increased receipts of the higher classes of passengers having been to no small extent counteracted by necessary increased expenditure in various directions. It may be frankly admitted that Indian railways are not adapted to cope with sudden and large demands for increased accommodation for the higher classes of passengers, and that it is on the third class, which provides nineteen-twentieths of the numbers carried and four-fifths of the receipts that the prosperity of this branch of the traffic depends. I may add that it is for its development and convenience that our attention should be specially directed."

Towards the close of 1901, Mr. Thomas Robertson, C.V.O., was deputed by the Secretary of State for India—

(1) To enquire into and report upon the administration and working of Indian railways, whether controlled by the State or by Companies, with special reference to the system under which they should be managed in India in the future;

(2) To report upon the feasibility of a systematic plan of railway development in India, to be worked up to by the Government over a series of years;

(3) To advise as to the management and development of the traffic, the convenience of the public and the improvement of the revenue, and

(4) Generally to make such suggestions as he might think useful for any or all of these purposes, including the extension of branches and light railways as feeders of the main line.

Mr. Robertson's report was issued in 1903, after he had travelled extensively over the Indian railways and investigated their general working and administration, and after he had visited America to study the methods of railway management there.

Mr. Robertson's general conclusion was that the "working of the Indian railways cannot be regarded as at all satisfactory," and that root and branch reform was needed; "if," he said, "the railways of India are to render that full and efficient service to the country of which they are capable, they must be permitted to be worked more as commercial enterprises than they have been in the past."

Mr. Robertson's report dealt in some detail with various questions of administration and working, criticised more particularly the

Government system of control and recommended its replacement by a Board composed of specially qualified railway men, who should be allowed to manage railway affairs entirely on commercial lines. Mr. Robertson also made certain suggestions as to the organisation of departments, salaries of officials and Home Board control. He compared State with Company management and advocated the transference of all lines to Companies. He dealt with the question of finance and commented upon railway working generally, making several proposals and suggestions, which will no doubt be given the consideration they deserve by the Board of Control since appointed by the Government of India. General Sir Richard Strachey made some interesting remarks on Mr. Robertson's report, which are here reproduced. Speaking at the general meeting held in June 1903, he said:—

"It will be of interest to you to know that the Government of India has published the report on the working of Indian railways, specially drawn up by Mr. Robertson, under the instructions of the Secretary of State, and has distributed copies to the various Railway Companies, apparently with the view of inviting opinion on the recommendations made in the report. I consequently feel in a measure bound to refer to it. While recognising that there is much in the report with which everyone conversant with the subject is likely to agree, and disclaiming any disposition to dogmatise on questions of administration, which no doubt involve many very complicated considerations, I may briefly state my personal conclusion that in this case, as in many others, it has been easier to point to defects than to suggest adequate remedies. That in some directions the system of Government administration may be improved I regard as indisputable. I fully concur with the report in describing the existing system of administration as 'cumbrous machinery, which is apt to impair the sense of responsibility, crush initiative, check progress and delay business to an extent which would be fatal to any other commercial enterprise.' Nor have I any difficulty in accepting the view that this is largely due to the fact that 'the administrative head of the department, namely, the member in charge of the Public Works Portfolio, has never had any previous training in railway working and management.' It might have been added that so far from the selection of this member of the Government being at present made on a consideration of any special aptitude for the discharge of his responsible duties, it is understood to be determined by some supposed established claim of the senior members of the Civil Service of the three old Presidencies of Bengal, Madras, and Bombay to obtain seats in the Governor-General's Council by a system of rotation.' In one of Lord Rosebery's recent speeches he remarked, when referring to the government of this country by Cabinets, 'that it works well on the whole is a tribute, less to the institution itself than to the capacity of our race to make any conceivable institution succeed.' With some hesitation as to the character of the results of the Government control of Indian railways, I think his remarks will well apply to it also.

At the same time, it appears impossible to deny that, notwithstanding what I am prepared to call very glaring defects, the general result of the treatment of railways in India considering the many serious difficulties that have been encountered, financial and administrative, has been remarkable, and the development of the present system of railways, extending to 26,000 miles, is highly creditable to those through whose exertions such a large measure of success has been obtained. I am therefore unable to accept, as justified by the actual results, the sweeping assertion of the report, that 'the present administration and working of the Indian railways cannot be regarded as at all satisfactory,' nor that 'root and branch reform alone will be productive of lasting good.' I see no reason for thinking that thoroughly qualified persons with adequate Indian experience may not be found to be entrusted with the management of the Public Works Department in India, in all its branches, as has been the case in all other branches of the administration, and in those cases has had the result of making Indian administration the admiration of all who have a real knowledge of what it is, and the difficulties it has to overcome.

The discussions that have taken place during the past year in this country as to the general character of English railway management, have not had the effect of showing satisfactorily any very remarkable superiority that it may possess over that of other countries, and this I am disposed to extend to India. I am unable to admit, for instance, that the management of a railway like the East Indian, which, mile for mile, carries without difficulty about eight times the number of passengers carried by the Illinois Central of the United States of America, and almost the same quantity of goods, and at rates not higher, with a net yearly profit to the Government, which owns the line, of something like a million sterling, after paying all charges for interest, and supplying a contribution of upwards of £400,000 towards the redemption of the original capital outlay, can be properly spoken of as calling for root and branch reform. I am, therefore, unable to see that the substitution of a body of English railway experts, with no knowledge of Indian conditions, is at all likely to supply what is wanted to produce satisfactory management of Indian railways, or that this is not to be obtained from persons trained in India itself.

I venture to say that the fundamental defects of the methods of control adopted by the Government of India arise from the inherent character of its bureaucratic organisation, which leads to a centralised system of intervention, extending to the smallest details of management, carried out through officials who are in many cases less competent to deal with the business in hand than those whose actions they control. It is, however, hardly possible to avoid the conclusion that the conditions of the contracts that exist between the Secretary of State and the Companies entrusted with the working of railways in India, render some such general system as that now in existence for the purpose of authorising expenditure essential, and so far as I am able to form an opinion, the objectionable friction that has often arisen in the case of this Company, to which alone my knowledge in this matter extends, has been caused by the mischievous tendency of the superior officers of the Government, to interfere with the discretion of the officers of the Company, rather than from the initiative of the consulting engineers, who communicate directly with the Company's officers, and are naturally animated by the spirit of their superiors

On this subject I will further only add that I can call to mind no case in which, in my judgment, has the Government control, *in recent times at all events,* conduced to 'prevent extravagance in construction, and subsequent waste in maintenance and working.' On the contrary, in many cases it has certainly led to results the reverse of this, by causing the postponement of works the construction of which might, with great advantage, have been taken up earlier, and by being distributed over a longer period have reduced the eventual pressure, financial and executive, which the growing urgent need of improvements has eventually rendered inevitable. Of the parts of the report that deal with questions of technical railway working, I do not think that I can usefully say more than that it is impossible to treat Indian railways as though they were all alike in their condition, and that to attempt to discuss details of this description on an occasion such as the present is out of the question, even if I were competent to offer opinions as to lines with the condition of which I have no specific knowledge."

Since these remarks were made, the Railway Board has been formed and now rules the destinies of the Railways in India.

In 1900 the work of removing the carriage and wagon building shops of the undertaking from Howrah to Lillooah was commenced. The move became necessary because of the cramped accommodation at Howrah, and because of the entry of the Bengal-Nagpur Railway into that terminus; but while the move was being effected the work of the Department naturally fell into arrears and when this happens it takes time to make up for lost way. Since then the construction of a new station for the joint use of the East Indian and Bengal-Nagpur Railways has been started and the portion so far sanctioned by the Government is now well on its way towards completion.

CHAPTER XXIX.

The East Indian Railway under Two Chairmen.

It has been said that the East Indian Railway has only had two Chairmen. As a matter of fact this is literally true, for the railway came into existence some years later than the Company, and though the Company has had four, the railway has only had two—Mr. Robert Wigram Crawford was appointed in 1854, immediately after the first section of the line had been opened for traffic, and when he died, in 1889, General Sir Richard Strachey succeeded him.

Mr. Crawford became Chairman of the Company at a time when, started as an experimental line, experience of the needs of the country and of trade requirements had to be gained by degrees; there was nothing to show what the possibilities were. Until trains actually began to run there were doubts whether the natives of India would travel by rail; until the railway was carried into the Raneegunge coal-field, Indian coal was practically unknown. It is true that before the days of railways, a certain quantity was brought down the Damoodar River from Raneegunge to Calcutta that, even up to the year 1859, the Bengal Coal Company were still boating coal, because the railway charges were too costly and the wagon stock insufficient; but this could only have been possible for a few months in the year, and profitable only when English coal was very scarce. Yet the fact remains that for several years after the opening of the railroad, the Bengal Coal Company found it necessary to employ a fleet of some 1,500 boats to bring their coal to market. Surely there could be no better proof than this of the unpreparedness of the railway to carry the traffic offering when it first opened, although it is recorded that in 1855 the railway "had contracted to convey 100,000 tons of coal from Raneegunge to Calcutta."

The export of grain and seeds from India to Europe was, at the time the railway opened, nominal, and whatever was exported came to the port by river. A trade in some items, which are now included among the principal staples carried, such as potatoes or kerosine oil, did not exist; cotton was the traffic which was expected to rank first in importance. "I go," said Lord Dalhousie on his appointment as Viceroy of India in 1847, "not to make wars but to send cotton home." India was behind all countries in which railroads had been constructed; Jamaica was the only place distant from Europe that could be pointed to as a precedent for the existence of a railway; it was at any rate the only place in which a railway existed, that was at all on a parallel with India. Had the East Indian Railway been completed to Delhi within ten years of the formation of the Company in 1845, as indeed it might well have been, if it had not been for the time lost in controversy and especially in coming to a final decision as to the route to be followed, the Indian Mutiny would have assumed a very different aspect. As it was it took so long to settle details that only the short length to Raneegunge had been constructed when the Mutiny broke out; yet even this short length proved of the greatest advantage to Government in helping forward troops and stores to the front.

Fortunately there were some far-seeing people who realized and insisted that there was in the construction of railways in India, even more than their strategic importance, even more than the primary idea of connecting the seat of the Supreme Government with the North-West Provinces. There were those, in short, who had the foresight and wisdom to see, that the development of the immense resources of the country could only be successfully effected by the introduction of a railroad system, and to believe with Lord Macaulay that, "excepting only the inventions of the alphabet and the printing press, none had done so much for the moral and intellectual progress of man as those *which* abridge distance and improve the means of communication." There was at least some truth in what a shareholder in the East Indian Railway remarked at the first meeting of the Board: "Railways would do more towards the civilization of India in seven years than all the missionaries had done in 200 years." But on the other hand there were many who held contrary views, and in the end the East Indian Railway was only sanctioned in part as an "experimental" line.

Among the pioneers of the East Indian Railway, the names of Mr. Crawford and Mr. Macdonald Stephenson will always be remembered. Both of them were associated with the undertaking from its inception; they were among the most prominent of those by whose exertions railways were first introduced into India. It was to Mr. Stephenson that the first steps in the construction and management of the East Indian Railway were entrusted, and his connection continued until 1892, when, owing to advanced age, he retired. Sir Macdonald Stephenson died shortly after his services with the Company were severed, and General Sir Richard Strachey, in referring to his death, remarked: "It does not fall to the lot of many to find their anticipations of success so fully realized as that achieved by the great undertaking, to the initiation of which Sir Macdonald Stephenson's perseverance and energy so largely contributed;

and the share he had in that result should always be remembered by those, who, like ourselves, are carrying on the work in which he so long participated."

To Mr. Crawford, however, must be given the credit for conducting the affairs of the Railway, not only up to the time of its purchase by Government, but for some nine years afterwards. Mr. Crawford had many difficulties to contend with, many obstacles to overcome, but he met them always with a sanguine mind and a perfect faith in ultimate success. If anything can be urged against Mr. Crawford, it was perhaps that he failed to realize, to its fullest extent, the part the railway should take in developing traffic. Rather than boldly reduce the coal tariff, Mr Crawford seemed to think that the East Indian Railway collieries could supply the railroads of India with fuel and that other collieries would develop of their own accord; while a reduction in third class fares was only introduced after the Government insisted on the measure. Still it must not be forgotten that, in those days, the first question of a railway man, in regard to any item of traffic was "what freight will it bear" instead of "at what cost can we carry it," and it is only natural that Mr. Crawford should have approached such problems with caution, though none knew better than he, the capabilities of the East Indian Railway to make a profit out of very low freights.

Then again, Mr. Crawford saw the traffic growing far more rapidly than the facilities of the railway, and there is little doubt that he was greatly handicapped by want of funds for improvements; the difficulties he had to contend with were in fact enormous. Almost at the outset of his career as Chairman, the outbreak of the mutiny in India may well have caused a panic among the shareholders in London, yet Mr. Crawford allayed their fears, by making a simple statement of the position, at a time when his heart must have been filled with knowledge that might have made the boldest quail. "The chief loss," he said, "will be that arising from the temporary stoppage of the principal portion of the works, and the consequent delay in their completion." These words were spoken within four months of the massacre at Cawnpore, where the blood of nearly all the East Indian Railway Engineers, engaged on the construction of the part of the line adjacent to that city, had been shed,* at a time of upheaval of the whole of India, and at a time when the Company's affairs in this country must have been in a state of chaos.

Mr. Crawford was Chairman of the Board of Directors from 1854 to 1889, and during these 35 years the gross receipts of the undertaking rose from a nominal sum to over

---

* Vide Appendix B.

four and a half crores of rupees in a year. During the next fourteen years, General Sir Richard Strachey saw a far more rapid development; the earnings rose to over four crores of rupees in half a year, and to nearly eight crores in a year.

When General Strachey succeeded Mr. Crawford as Chairman, the East Indian Railway controlled 1,626 miles. During the preceding ten years there had practically been no addition to the length of line worked; want of funds had prevented extensions, if indeed their importance had been thoroughly recognised. The undertaking had, as a matter of fact, remained in a state of torpor; from the time the Chord line was completed, it had not made any real progress. It is true that its traffic had continued to grow, but the growth, viewed in the light of what followed, had been very gradual, and in regard to improvements only the most urgent and pressing needs had been provided for.

During the next fifteen years, the mileage worked increased to $2,241\frac{3}{4}$ miles, while at their close the Grand Chord line, the Shikohabad-Farrukabad extension (since completed), the Ondal-Sainthea Chord, the Khurja-Hapur branch and Bhagulpur-Bausi Railway, each in itself a considerable undertaking, were all under construction. Mr. Crawford's period of Chairmanship marked the completion of an idea. General Sir Richard Strachey's tenure marked an extension of that idea, an extension, such as had not entered into the conception of the originators of the railway.

In the year 1889 when General Strachey became Chairman of the East Indian Railway, the Government share of the surplus profits was Rs. 33,25,385, and the Company's share Rs. 9,44,812. In 1904, the Government share amounted to Rs. 1,88,99,860, and the Company's share to Rs. 21,05,027. The terms of the contract under which the Company works the railway for the Government have, during the Chairmanship of General Sir Richard Strachey, been made far more favourable to Government, still the dividend to the shareholders, or, as they now are, the Deferred Annuitants, is greater than it was in 1889, although, be it remembered, the rate of exchange is lower. In 1889, when General Strachey became Chairman, with exchange at more than 1-5d. per rupee, the dividend paid was £5-0-6, per cent, in 1904 with exchange at 1-4d. the dividend was £6-2-0. per cent. It is doubtful whether in the world's history an undertaking of such magnitude as the East Indian Railway has proved so great a success, both financially and otherwise. The capital outlay on the East Indian Railway Company which was in 1850 three millions sterling, rose by the end of 1904 to more than thirty-three and a half millions sterling, and so large are the additions now being made to the locomotive and rolling stock, and so great is the cost of the additions and improvements to way and works, to stations and buildings, to the Company's collieries, workshops and so forth, which are constantly being carried out, that the half-yearly outlay on capital account has for some years been about five hundred thousand pounds. The staff has been greatly augmented, and the Traffic Department in particular has recently been reorganized. In a word, no effort has been spared in making the East Indian foremost of all railways in India, while it retains the unique position of being the cheapest worked line of its size in the world.

The difficulty of obtaining funds for the construction of extensions, for additions to rolling stock, and for the improvement of facilities generally, has been one of the greatest with which General Sir Richard Strachey has had to contend during his Chairmanship. As he remarked in 1890: "The fact that the sum allowed for the coming year for capital outlay is restricted to three lakhs, and granted with the admonition that if possible less is to be spent, is an illustration of this position. I must be allowed to say that such a grant for a railway extending over 1,500 miles and representing a capital of about 50 crores of rupees, is hardly more than illusory."

It was not until 1897 that the funds available for capital expenditure were sufficient to render anything like active progress possible. The Moghalsarai-Gya line, with the branch to Daltongunge was then undertaken, as a first instalment of the Grand Chord. In the succeeding five years there was an average yearly capital outlay of 157 lakhs of rupees, all of which was devoted to construction, to additional engines and rolling stock, and to improvements on the line, including station buildings, staff quarters, workshops and other permanent works. But as before indicated, from 1880 to 1890 the capital outlay had been nominal, the East Indian Railway had been allowed to remain in a condition of torpor. All this had to be remedied and it was General Sir Richard Strachey who had to find the remedy.

When General Strachey became Chairman, the experimental stage had passed away, the success of the railway had become assured. It remained to him to develop what had been created, to make the progress of the future worthy of the success of the past. There are few who will dispute that his policy in reducing rates, particularly the coal rates, his great foresight, and unique knowledge of detail, added to his vast experience and intimate connection with India, have in no small measure contributed to the immense development of traffic which has taken place in the last few years.

It was of him that his brother wrote: "There are, in my belief, few men living who have done so much, often in ways unknown to the outside world, for the improvement of Indian administration. It is to him that India owes the initiation of that great policy of the systematic extension of railways and canals which has been crowned with such extraordinary success, which has increased to an incalculable extent the wealth of the country, and has profoundly altered its condition. To him is due the conception of those measures of financial and administrative decentralisation which have had the most far-reaching consequences, and which were pronounced by Sir Henry Maine to be by far the greatest and most successful reforms carried out in India in his time. To his active support is largely due the initiation of the measures, which have proved of the highest value, for preventing the destruction of the Indian forests, and for their scientific protection and management. He it was who first organised the great Department of Public Works, and laid the foundations of the scientific study of Indian meteorology. He was the first, many years ago, to advise that reform of the currency which has now been carried out and the delay of which has involved India in incalculable loss."*

It may not be out of place here to relate a short story about General Sir Richard

---

* "India, its Administration and Progress," by Sir John Strachey.

Strachey. When he took to Lord Lawrence for signature, the great despatch on the policy of the Government borrowing largely for reproductive public works, of which of course he had written every word himself, Lord Lawrence put his " L " to the foot of it, and as he laid down his pen looked at General Strachey with a grin and said " They will think me very clever. " So, indeed, would many be thought who could sign, as their own, despatches written by the hand of the Chairman of the East Indian Railway.

These remarks would be very incomplete without a word of reference to one, who has been intimately associated with the undertaking for the past fifty years, and still retains his close connection with all its affairs ; one who may indeed be regarded as the doyen of the Railway Company and the right-hand man of both its Chairmen ; I refer to Sir Alexander Rendel, the Company's Consulting Engineer.

Part only of Sir Alexander Rendel's work is referred to in this volume, it would form a history in itself to detail it in full, but if asked to point to the most important measure introduced by him (in conjunction with General Strachey, years before he became Chairman of the East Indian Railway), I would mention railway statistics. Undoubtedly these were initiated by him and afterwards became a most valuable guide to the proper conduct of railways and the chief basis for economies in working.

Just one word more. It is the administrative and executive staff in India who have to bear the heat and burden of the day, and the Board of Directors have never had cause to regret the confidence they have invariably placed in the loyal support and co-operation of the workers in India. From the humble porter to the Agent of the Company, every servant of the railway has a task to fulfil; each day brings its round of toil, a difficulty to be overcome, possibly a danger to be faced. The part taken by its employés in this country, in furthering the success of the great undertaking cannot be minimised, and both Chairmen have been among the first to recognise this. Long may it be so, for such recognition is as well deserved now as it was in the early days, when the Government of India lost no opportunity of eulogising the work done by the servants of the Company, though similar work done now is often regarded as a matter of course.

APPENDIX A.

LIST OF AGENTS OR CHAIRMEN OF BOARD OF AGENCY.

Names.	Term of Service.
Mr. R. Macdonald Stephenson	1853—1857
,, Edward Palmer	1857—1873
,, Cecil Stephenson	1873—1875
Sir Bradford Leslie, K.C.I.E.	1876—1887
Mr. D. W. Campbell, C.I.E.	1887—1891
Col. R. Gardiner, R.E.	1891—1899
Mr. James Douglas	1899— ...

SECRETARIES TO AGENT.

Names.	Term of Service.
Mr. Cecil Stephenson	1858—1865
,, T. Lovelock	1866—1872
,, W. H. Russell	1872—1878
,, P. Wagstaff	1878—1900
,, H. Wood	1900— ...

CHIEF ENGINEERS.

Names.	Term of Service.
Mr. G. Turnbull	1850—1863
,, S. Power	1863—1868
,, *G. Sibley	1862—1876
,, Sir B. Leslie, K.C.I.E.	1876—1882
,, C. H. Denham	1882—1889
,, F. E. Robertson, C.I.E.	1889—1897
,, E. H. Stone	1897—1903
,, C. F. Findlay	1903—1903
,, R. S. Highet	1903— ...

* From 1862 to 1868 he was Chief Engineer, Upper Provinces, with head-quarters at Allahabad.

Chief Auditors.

Names.	Term of Service.
Mr. Rob Roberts	1863—1877
„ R. C. S. Mackenzie	1877—1892
„ J. Douglas	1893—1899
„ T. Bashford	1899— …

General Traffic Managers.

Names.	Term of Service.
Mr. F. Cox	1858—1859
„ J. C. Batchelor*	1860—1879
„ N. St. L. Carter	1879—1891
„ J. M. Rutherford	1891—1897
„ W. A. Dring	1897— …

* Mr. Batchelor took charge of the entire line from 1st January 1866. Before this Mr. B. P. W. Smyth was Traffic Manager, Allahabad, and Mr. Batchelor was Traffic Manager, Howrah.

Locomotive Superintendents.

Names.	Term of Service.
Mr. J. Hodgson	1855—1857
„ Lingard Stokes	1857—1863
„ D. W. Campbell	1863—1887
„ J. Strachan	1887—1890
„ A. W. Rendell	1890—1901
„ T. R. Browne	1901— …

Mr. P. D. Nicholl was Locomotive Superintendent, Upper Provinces, with head-quarters at Allahabad, before Mr. D. W. Campbell.

Carriage and Wagon Superintendents.

Names.	Term of Service.
Mr. R. W. Pearce	1862—1889
„ Richard Pearce	1889—1898
„ T. R. Brown	1899—1901
„ H. K. Bamber, M.V.O.	1901— …

COLLIERY SUPERINTENDENTS.

Names.	Term of Service.
Mr. J. F. Cockburn (Resdt. Engr.)	1859—1871
,, T. E. Dunn	1871—1876
,, I. J. Whitty	1876—1879
,, R. H. Abbatt	1879—1880
,, W. G. Olpherts	1880—1881
,, Dr. W. Saise	1881—1905
,, T. H. Ward	1905— ...

In 1863 the mining operations in the Giridih colliery having been suspended, all establishment was reduced to that required to guard the property, till a suitable branch railway was established.

CHIEF MEDICAL OFFICERS.

Names.	Term of Service.
Mr. R. G. Griffith	1893—1902
,, J. S. Brooke	1902— ...

HEADS OF STORE DEPARTMENT.

Names.	Term of Service.
Mr. T. F. Campbell (General Storekeeper)	1858—1860
,, D. Murray (Do.)	1860—1862
,, A. C. Bell (Principal Store-keeper)	1863—1864
,, G. H. W. Conroy (Chief Storekeeper)	1864—1883
,, *J. Oates (Controller of Stores)	1883—1898
,, W. Humphries Do.	1898—1902
,, T. A. White Do	1903— ...

* From 1886 the designation was changed to Controller of Stores.

APPENDIX B.

The following is a copy of the Inscription on the Memorial Tablet in Cawnpore Church :—

TO THE MEMORY OF THE ENGINEERS IN THE SERVICE OF THE EAST INDIAN RAILWAY COMPANY,

WHO DIED, AND WERE KILLED, IN THE GREAT INSURRECTION OF 1857.

JOHN HODGSON, LOCOMOTIVE SUPERINTENDENT, DIED AT ALLAHABAD, JUNE 21ST.

R. N. MANTELL, DISTRICT ENGINEER, DIED AT ALLAHABAD, JUNE 30TH.

A. M. M. MILLER, RESIDENT ENGINEER, KILLED AT CAWNPORE, JUNE 27TH.

A. C. HEBERDEN, RESIDENT ENGINEER, KILLED AT CAWNPORE, JUNE 27TH.

W. DIGGES LATOUCHE, ASSISTANT ENGINEER, KILLED AT CAWNPORE, JUNE 27TH.

ROBERT HANNA, ASSISTANT ENGINEER, KILLED AT CAWNPORE, JUNE 27TH.

J. C. BAYNE, ASSISTANT ENGINEER, KILLED AT CAWNPORE, JUNE 27TH.

THOMAS BYRNE, ASSISTANT ENGINEER, DIED AT CALCUTTA, JULY.

Breinigsville, PA USA
21 March 2011
258086BV00005B/94/P